HOW TO PLAY THE WORLD'S MOST EXCLUSIVE GOLF CLUBS

A Journey through Pine Valley, Royal Melbourne, Augusta, Muirfield, and More

By John Sabino

Skyhorse Publishing

Skyhorse Publishing books may be purchased in bulk at special discounts for sales promotion, corporate gifts, fund-raising, or educational purposes. Special editions can also be created to specifications. For details, contact the Special Sales Department, Skyhorse Publishing, 307 West 36th Street, 11th Floor, New York, NY 10018 or info@skyhorsepublishing.com.

Skyhorse® and Skyhorse Publishing® are registered trademarks of Skyhorse Publishing, Inc.®, a Delaware corporation.

Visit our website at www.skyhorsepublishing.com.

10 9 8 7 6 5 4 3 2 1

Library of Congress Cataloging-in-Publication Data is available on file.

All interior photographs by John Sabino, unless otherwise noted.

Cover design by Tom Lau
Cover photo credit John Sabino

ISBN: 978-1-63450-799-8
Ebook ISBN: 978-1-63450-805-6

Printed in China

To Brianne and Brian.

Contents

"Life must be lived forwards, but understood backwards."

—Søren Kierkegaard

SECTION I
Laying the Groundwork and Basic Methods

CHAPTER ONE
Background and Introduction

Obsessed beyond all reason, I had become Captain Ahab, and Augusta National, my Moby Dick. The ultimate prize for any golfer who loves the game is playing Augusta and I was repeatedly turned away in my attempts to play. I was determined to one day put my tee into the lush grass on the first tee and hit my drive down the fairway.

Several years ago I set out on a quixotic journey to play the top 100 ranked golf courses in the world. My endeavor was both exhilarating and difficult, because many of the courses are located in remote locations, have small memberships, are publicity shy, and sometimes do not openly welcome guests. As one of a handful of golfers fortunate enough to have completed this quest, I have picked up some insights along the way about how to access some of the most exclusive golf clubs in the world.

My own journey began twelve years ago when a friend gave me a wooden "peg" board which contained the rankings of the top 100 courses. Next to each course name was a hole you insert a small peg into after completing the course. At the time I received it, I had already played about twenty courses on the list, mostly resort courses and courses in Scotland and Ireland I had played on golf trips with friends. I consider myself goal oriented and I thought, as a stretch goal, maybe I could play all 100. As goal-oriented and anal-retentive people do, I started to map out a strategy of how I

The "peg" board.

could play the courses. I put together a list, built a spreadsheet, imagined some ways I might be able to play the courses, and I was off on my fanciful journey.

A couple of years into the quest I started writing a blog as a way to remember the places I visited. The pilgrimage was best summed up by the simple four-word tagline I gave it: "Pursuing Golf's Holy Grail." The blog gained momentum, and with a couple of friends I began to slowly tick off courses. Ultimately, my blog attracted over one million readers and many people along the way told me I should write a book about the experience, although I didn't give it much thought. Now that the journey is complete, the most frequent question I am asked is, "How did you get on all these courses?" The other common query I get is, "How did you get on Augusta?" Through my journey I have come to know ten people who have completed the same challenge and they all say the same thing: everyone wants to know how they were able to play Augusta.

Writing the blog was entertaining, but the idea of a book didn't hold much appeal to me. Several people who have played top courses in the United States self-published books, but I wasn't attracted to the genre since no one—well, maybe my mother— wants a blow-by-blow of my trips or cares what score I shot. I didn't want to do another me-too book. But when an experienced publisher contacted me and came up with an interesting twist, I was intrigued. Why not write the book from the perspective of the reader: What's in it for them? How can someone else play some of these courses?

The golf world is made up of people who are benevolent in many ways; now, it is my turn to give back to a game that has given me so much by passing along the methods and techniques I used to play the world's great golf courses. How do you play at the upper echelon of clubs in the world? In the end, it is simple. All you need is the time, the resources, and the connections; although there are exceptions, since I played several top courses for free and without connections.

The focus of the book will be insights into how I gained access to the clubs and techniques you can use if you have a desire to play some of these world-class courses. It will include some wisdom I gained from the journey and interesting stories about others who have pursued similar journeys. Although I won't focus on many courses in detail, there are some special clubs I think warrant a more intimate look and in a small number of cases I will delve into noteworthy golf holes.

My journey followed the 80/20 rule—about 80 percent of the courses I played, while spectacular, do not offer a compelling or interesting story to most people. No disrespect at all is intended to the collection of fabulous courses I won't elaborate on; however, the sizzle in the story are the trips to Paris, Scotland, and some other one-of-a-kind locations.

How and Why?

Although I use the top 100 courses as a starting point, I also looked at other criteria as I compiled my personal list of the most exclusive, and I am giving myself wide latitude to be judge and jury when determining which clubs to include or exclude in the book; the only certainty is not everyone will agree with my choices.

I have organized the book into categories based on how difficult each course is to access from my point of view and experience. Some of the best in the world are easy to play if you have the time, money, and the freedom to travel. Others are halfway or all the way around the world and you need to be invited by a member who speaks a foreign language. Most are somewhere in between. And then there is Augusta, which is in a league of its own and by far the most difficult course in the world to gain access to; although, as you will see, there are many ways to play the course if you are determined—or manic—enough.

Some of the advice I have is basic. You have to network and find people who are members of clubs or who can introduce you to members. You also need to be opportunistic; if you are invited to play an exclusive golf course, rearrange your schedule and go do it since you never know if and when the opportunity might arise again. There are many courses I only had one chance to play, and if I didn't jump at the opportunity I would still be waiting. I was incredibly lucky throughout my journey and will show you some of the ways you can improve your luck, which can have a positive impact in life and in trying to play your dream golf courses.

From those in the critic category, I can hear the howls rising. This spoiled prima donna is writing a book to show other fat cats how to do something elitist; how obnoxious. Maybe. Although, I am not fat and I started with little and have done all right in this world and success is nothing to apologize for. I truly feel part of what makes golf great is its honorable traditions. You observe the rules, call penalties on yourself, show proper etiquette, and have respect for the game and your fellow golfers. Golf gives back to the community and golfers I have met are a generous lot; the PGA tour gives money to charity every week; pro-ams support worthy causes, and many of these elite clubs sponsor caddie scholarships or help underprivileged kids or other important causes. To emphasize the point, I am giving my share of the proceeds from writing the book to charities benefiting children.

The Goal

There is a growing fraternity of golf fanatics who have set goals to play exclusive golf courses. My own goal was the top 100 ranked courses in the world, which I achieved using the *Golf Magazine* 2003 rankings. Their particular list changes every two years; other golfers who have completed playing the top 100 in the world have played lists from different years. Some have tried (or have played) all the courses *ever* ranked in the top 100, some have played the top 100 courses in the United States, others in England or New Zealand. Regardless of your personal goal, even if it is simply to one day play at Pine Valley or Riviera, you will nevertheless find the book useful and hopefully entertaining. Likewise, if you are an armchair traveler who doesn't play and wants some intriguing stories of life, travel, golf, and insights into some elite clubs, I have worked hard to make the story worthy of your time.

Looking back, the genesis of the book was solidified on a fairy-tale day in April of 2013 when an unlikely birdie putt dropped, but more about that later.

The Elevated Profile of Golf Clubs

While some of the world's greatest golf clubs have existed for a long time, there are five factors that have come together over the last thirty years to raise their profiles and have fueled the desire for people to play them. The first influencing factor is the advent of cheap air travel since the 1970s, which makes it easy to reach the courses.

The second is the launch and continued evolution of golf course ratings by golf magazines. *Golf Digest* highlighted "America's Greatest Golf Courses" in 1966 and published a book called *Great Golf Courses of the World* in 1974. *Golf Magazine* joined the fray and went global by publishing their first list of the top fifty courses in the world in 1979; then in 1982 they expanded the list to 100 courses. Today these two magazines continue to publish revised ratings biennially. They have been joined by *Golfweek Magazine* and *Links Magazine,* who publish various lists and rankings. Each magazine uses their own formula to rate courses; *Golf Magazine* has 100 panelists who are well-known PGA tour players, golf course architects, course owners, USGA dignitaries, and others of distinction in the industry; people such as Gary Player, Frank Nobilo, Tom Weiskopf, Tom Doak, and David Fay. *Golf Digest* takes a different approach in its rating panel and uses a larger group—1,000 raters—of low-handicap golfers; *Golfweek* has a more eclectic group of raters.

At the end of the day, the ranking methodologies are subjective and relative. There are endless arguments about which courses are best, which are overrated, and which are underrated. Try doing a rating exercise yourself and see how you make out. Write down what you think the best twenty-five courses are, then put the list aside and do it again a month later without looking at your original list. It is likely the list will not be the same. Part of what makes the study and appreciation of these clubs and courses so interesting is this comparative aspect of it: Which is your favorite course? Which is the most difficult? Which would you go out of your way to play? Even with all the variation in the methodologies and lists, the top fifty or so courses in the world are generally agreed upon and tend to change very little.

The third factor is the rising prominence of technology; in particular, websites dedicated to the study of golf course architecture, specifically GolfClubAtlas.com, which profiles notable courses. Seeing vivid color images of Sand Hills or Maidstone on these sites provides all the inspiration needed to make you want to go and play them. The rise of blogs and social media have also allowed the sharing of information to proliferate, and technology makes it easier to find courses, network with a member, or book a tee time.

The fourth factor is the general rise and visibility of the game attributable to Tiger Woods. We are lucky to live in the Tiger era, as most of the top professionals in the

Maidstone Club, East Hampton, 14th hole.

game acknowledge. As a result of his presence, the purses are higher and there is more television coverage and interest in the game; thus, the profile of top courses and clubs has been raised.

The fifth factor is a result of the age we live in—a new Golden Age of golf course architecture. The 1920s were the first Golden Age and about a third of the now-acknowledged best courses and clubs were built in or around that era. The last twenty to twenty-five years have seen a resurgence in golf courses being built, fueled by global bull markets and a general rise in prosperity at the high end. It has created enormous sums of wealth, enabling places such as Sebonack, the Bandon Resort, Friar's Head, Nine Bridges, and a multitude of other top clubs and courses to be built. The general appreciation of golf is enhanced by these new courses, and you are excited to play more when you see how enjoyable a club is or when you experience architecture that inspires you.

We also live in a ratings-filled society. A generation ago you could enjoy a nice bottle of wine without giving it further thought; now you drink a bottle rated 93 by

Robert Parker and the restaurant you frequent has a Zagat's food rating of 25. A more direct analogy relates to college rankings; magazines now rank colleges and universities in the same manner golf magazines rank golf courses. *Forbes* says Stanford is the number one business school and *U.S. News* says it's Wharton, and on it goes. Before, you enjoyed playing a challenging golf course; now you want to play the number three ranked course in the world.

Exclusivity

So what exactly makes a golf course or club exclusive? There is no simple answer but there are a number of factors that go into it; one is age and heritage. The Royal & Ancient Golf Club of St. Andrews was started in 1754, the Honourable Company of Edinburgh Golfers began ten years before. In golf, age is tradition. Early clubs are highly regarded, especially those that helped establish the rules and traditions, and not only those in the home of golf in Scotland. The Chicago Golf Club and the Country Club in Brookline, Massachusetts, were early clubs in the United States and founding members of the USGA, which gives them prestige and pedigree.

The history of a club is an important factor in determining exclusivity. Ben Hogan used to practice at the Colonial Country Club in Fort Worth and is closely associated with it. Bobby Jones played his golf growing up at the East Lake Golf Club in Atlanta, making it one of the most revered places in the game. Harry Vardon was the professional at the Ganton Golf Club for many years, and James Braid was the same at Walton Heath. When legendary golfers are affiliated with a club it enhances its prestige.

The designer—or golf course architect—is an important factor as well. Charles Blair Macdonald, the driving force behind the founding of the USGA and the designer of the National Golf Links of America is one of the premier architects ever to have lived. Courses he was involved in have automatic prestige; the same for Alister MacKenzie, designer of Royal Melbourne and Cypress Point, and co-designer of Augusta National with Bobby Jones. There are certain brand-name architects that confer a course instant appeal—designers such as H. S. Colt, Seth Raynor, A. W. Tillinghast, Tom Simpson, Stanley Thompson, Old Tom Morris, C. H. Alison, and Donald Ross.

In the modern era, those of Tom Doak and the design team of Bill Coore and Ben Crenshaw are reaching similar levels of respect. A pedigreed designer isn't a guarantee of greatness, though, since Donald Ross was involved in hundreds of courses, and only a small minority are world-ranked.

Location can sometimes be an important factor, especially clubs located on dramatic land near the sea, such as Pebble Beach and Cypress Point in Northern California, Old Head in Ireland, and Cruden Bay and Turnberry in Scotland. Or, the spectacular piece of property with its dramatic headlands occupied by the New South Wales Golf Club near Sydney, where Captain Cook anchored when he visited Australia for the first time.

A course or club that has hosted a major championship tends to be more highly regarded, particularly those that have done so multiple times such as Merion, Oakmont, the Country Club, Royal St. George's, and Royal Liverpool.

Newer clubs do not always have these factors but it can be the exclusivity itself that makes them prestigious. The Loch Lomond Golf Club in Scotland, a global "destination club" with limited membership, is a leading example. Psychology is such that people often want what they can't have. Tell a child they can't have something and what do they do? They want it more. Tell the elite you're limiting membership to 150 people and invite a couple of über-golfers to join; this exclusivity creates demand and people are drawn to it. Especially because at most of these clubs being a member is all about who you know, not about how big a check you can stroke.

Sometimes the uniqueness of the clubhouse is a factor, although it would be a stretch to say this alone makes it exclusive. Prominent examples include the eighteenth-century Georgian mansion Rossdhu House at Loch Lomond, and in New York, the Stanford White designed Shinnecock Hills shingle-style clubhouse in Southampton, and the McKim, Mead & White designed clubhouse at Sleepy Hollow, whose grounds were laid out by the landscape architect of Central Park, Frederick Law Olmsted. Sometimes it is the aura and reputation of the locker room that creates a buzz, most notably at Seminole near Palm Beach, although, clearly, the clubhouse or locker room in isolation is not an important enough factor to make a club preeminent; it is the multiplicity of factors that makes the great ones truly great. The National Golf

Clubhouse, Seminole Golf Club, Florida.

Links has one of the most impressive clubhouses in the world, a breathtaking setting on Peconic Bay, a pedigreed designer, and it hosted the first Walker Cup, which Bobby Jones played in. In addition to its locker room, Seminole was founded by E. F. Hutton, Ben Hogan used it as a hangout before the Masters each year, John F. Kennedy visited, the course was designed by Donald Ross, and it sits on the Atlantic Ocean. Augusta National Golf Club similarly checks all the boxes, and more.

Sometimes it is the intangibles that make a club exclusive. There are a select few courses that are unforgettable because the course is so exhilarating and awe-inspiring, and it stirs the soul to a degree that when you stand on most tees you say out loud, "Wow." The truly elite possess unique charms in addition to their world-class golf courses; be it the isolated and down-to-earth atmosphere at Sand Hills in Nebraska with its rustic cabins and lunar feel, or Merion's reserved ambiance, signature turtle soup, historic locker room, and oversized showerheads. Or, the tradition of wearing a jacket and tie at Royal St. George's and its associations with the British aristocracy. In the end, what makes these places worth seeking out cannot always be articulated clearly but can be summed up succinctly in the words of Justice Potter Stewart, who said, "You know it when you see it." Justice Stewart was referring to pornography at the time, but it applies equally well to an exclusive golf club.

The Entry Gate at Yeamans Hall Club, Charleston.

Golf Magazine's 2003 list of the Top 100 Golf Courses in the World

1. Pine Valley, Clementon, New Jersey (1918)	21. Kingston Heath, Cheltenham, Australia (1925)
2. Cypress Point, Pebble Beach, California (1928)	22. Seminole, North Palm Beach, Florida (1929)
3. Muirfield, Gullane, Scotland (1891)	23. Prairie Dunes, Hutchinson, Kansas (1935)
4. Shinnecock Hills, Southampton, New York (1931)	24. Crystal Downs, Frankfort, Michigan (1929)
5. Augusta National, Augusta, Georgia (1932)	25. Oakland Hills (South), Bloomfield Hills, Michigan (1917)
6. The Old Course, St. Andrews, Scotland (16th Century)	26. Carnoustie, Carnoustie, Scotland (1842)
7. Pebble Beach, Pebble Beach, California (1919)	27. San Francisco Golf, San Francisco, California (1915)
8. Royal Melbourne (Composite), Australia (1926)	28. Royal Birkdale, Southport, England (1889)
9. Pinehurst No. 2, Pinehurst, North Carolina (1903–1935)	29. Fishers Island, Fishers Island, New York (1917)
10 Royal County Down, Newcastle, Northern Ireland (1889)	30. Bethpage (Black), Farmingdale, New York (1936)
11. Sand Hills, Mullen, Nebraska (1995)	31. Chicago Golf, Wheaton, Illinois (1895)
12. Royal Portrush (Dunluce), Northern Ireland (1929)	32. Royal St. George's, Sandwich, England (1887)
13. Ballybunion Old, Ballybunion, Ireland (1906)	33. The Country Club, Brookline, Massachusetts (1895)
14. Merion (East), Ardmore, Pennsylvania (1912)	34. Casa de Campo, La Romana, Dominican Republic (1971)
15. Oakmont, Oakmont, Pennsylvania (1903)	35. Hirono, Kobe, Japan (1932)
16. Royal Dornoch, Dornoch, Scotland (1886)	36. Riviera, Pacific Palisades, California (1926)
17. Turnberry (Ailsa), Turnberry, Scotland (1906)	37. Muirfield Village, Dublin, Ohio (1974)
18. Winged Foot (West), Mamaroneck, New York (1923)	38. Royal Troon (Old), Troon, Scotland (1878)
19. Pacific Dunes, Bandon, Oregon (2001)	39. Olympic (Lake), San Francisco, California (1917)
20. National Golf Links of America, Southampton, New York (1911)	40. Portmarnock, Portmarnock, Ireland (1894)

41. Southern Hills, Tulsa, Oklahoma (1935)	62. Ganton, Ganton, England (1891)
42. Oak Hill (East), Rochester, New York (1926)	63. Camargo, Cincinnati, Ohio (1921)
43. New South Wales, La Perouse, Australia (1928)	64. Highlands Links, Nova Scotia, Canada (1935)
44. Sunningdale (Old), Sunningdale, England (1901)	65. Kingsbarns, St. Andrews, Scotland (1999)
45. Baltusrol (Lower), Springfield, New Jersey (1922)	66. Winged Foot (East), Mamaroneck, New York (1923)
46. Woodhall Spa, Woodhall Spa, England (1905)	67. Harbour Town, Hilton Head Island, South Carolina (1969)
47. Morfontaine, Senlis, France (1927)	68. Cabo del Sol (Ocean), Los Cabos, Mexico (1994)
48. The Golf Club, New Albany, Ohio (1967)	69. Somerset Hills, Bernardsville, New Jersey (1917)
49. Kauri Cliffs, Kaeo, New Zealand (2000)	70. Durban, Durban, South Africa (1922)
50. Royal Adelaide, Adelaide, Australia (1904)	71. Scioto, Columbus, Ohio (1916)
51. Shoreacres, Lake Bluff, Illinois (1919)	72. Royal Liverpool, Hoylake, England (1869)
52. Medinah (No. 3), Medinah, Illinois (1928)	73. Lahinch, Lahinch, Ireland (1893)
53. Whistling Straits (Straits), Haven, Wisconsin (1998)	74. Bandon Dunes, Bandon, Oregon (1999)
54. Royal Lytham & St. Annes, Lytham St. Annes, England (1886)	75. Naruo, Osaka, Japan (1904)
55. Garden City, Garden City, New York (1898)	76. Cruden Bay, Cruden Bay, Scotland (1926)
56. Loch Lomond, Luss, Scotland (1994)	77. Valderrama, Sotogrande, Spain (1975)
57. TPC Sawgrass (Stadium), Ponte Vedra, Florida (1981)	78. Wentworth (West), Virginia Water, England (1924)
58. Inverness, Toledo, Ohio (1919)	79. Kiawah Island (Ocean), Kiawah Island, South Carolina (1991)
59. Los Angeles (North), Los Angeles, California (1921)	80. Kawana (Fuji), Kawana, Japan (1936)
60. Maidstone, East Hampton, New York (1891)	81. Spyglass Hill, Pebble Beach, California (1966)
61. Quaker Ridge, Scarsdale, New York (1926)	82. Walton Heath (Old), Tadworth, England (1904)

83. World Woods (Pine Barrens), Florida (1993)	92. Yeamans Hall, Hanahan, South Carolina (1925)
84. Ocean Forest, Sea Island, Georgia (1995)	93. El Saler, Valencia, Spain (1967)
85. Valley Club of Montecito, Santa Barbara, California (1928)	94. Homestead (Cascades), Hot Springs, Virginia (1923)
86. Congressional (Blue), Bethesda, Maryland (1924)	95. St. George's, Etobicoke, Ontario, Canada (1929)
87. Peachtree, Atlanta, Georgia (1948)	96. The Honors Course, Ooltewah, Tennessee (1984)
88. Wade Hampton, Cashiers, North Carolina (1987)	97. East Lake, Atlanta, Georgia (1910)
89. Shadow Creek, North Las Vegas, Nevada (1989)	98. The European Club, Brittas Bay, Ireland (1992)
90. Cherry Hills, Cherry Hills, Colorado (1923)	99. Paraparaumu Beach, Paraparaumu Beach, New Zealand (1949)
91. Baltimore (Five Farms), Lutherville, Maryland (1926)	100. Colonial, Fort Worth, Texas (1935)

CHAPTER TWO

Accessing Golf Clubs in the Facebook Era

Technology can be a valuable resource as you try to find a way to play an exclusive golf club. First and foremost you can go to the club's website to learn more about it, such as their guest policies and their history. This is particularly helpful for private clubs outside the United States, which typically allow guests on certain dates and times. One of the first lessons to learn as you find your way around the world of elite clubs is, the more exclusive the club, generally, the less they have a web presence. Some of the toniest have no web presence at all, including the Chicago Golf Club, Cypress Point, Pine Valley, Seminole, and the Valley Club of Montecito. Others, including the trio of courses in the Hamptons—the National Golf Links, Maidstone, and Shinnecock Hills—have the merest presences of all, mostly a splash page and a login area for members, and that's all. This signals to the outside world they are content with their privacy and do not welcome unaccompanied guests.

Other good resources are websites that profile courses, such as www.top100golf-courses.co.uk, which can give you a good feel for many clubs around the world and provides some basic history and background. Darius Oliver's website, www.planetgolf.com, based on his books of the same name, is also valuable.

Aside from doing a Google search on a club, you can also set up a "Google Alert" that will send you an email any time the subject of your search matches. For example, if you are interested in keeping track of news related to the Prairie Dunes Country Club

Cypress Point Club, Pebble Beach, California.

in Kansas, you can establish a Google Alert for "Prairie Dunes" and you will receive an email whenever a news item or new web reference is made about the course. Google can be useful to find out whether a course or club has any charity outings; the most august golf clubs in the world, such as Shinnecock Hills and the Olympic Club in San Francisco, host charity outings. Even if the results that come up are for prior outings, most hold events annually to raise money for good causes, so if the club hosted an event in the past, the odds are good they will hold one in the future. A good way to keep up to date on this is to setup your Google Alert so it includes the words "Charity Outing."

Charitybuzz.com is an additional tool which promotes charitable auctions across the United States. They feature all types of events, with access to Hollywood stars, restaurants, and a variety of entertainment areas. And, they have a golf section. Because the website has broad appeal, the auction prices tend to be relatively high; however, sought-after clubs are offered throughout the year. Although Charitybuzz.com is a good resource to keep in touch with what is going on nationally, you can probably bid on a threesome or foursome cheaper at a local charity auction.

You can use GolfVacationInsider.com as another method to find rounds being auctioned for charity at various high-end clubs. Its sister site GolfOdyssey.com requires a subscription, but has broader content and is pithy and smartly written; it frequently has useful tips on how to access courses and other items of interest to the traveling golfer. Additionally, look at your local golf association or regional websites; for example, the website of Play Golf Minnesota lists charity outings at some historic and well-known clubs, as does the Long Island Golf News, which highlights some hard-to-access courses hosting charity outings.

Prairie Dunes, Hutchinson, Kansas, 8th Fairway.

I mentioned GolfClubAtlas.com in the opening chapter. Its gifted creator has a knack for profiling courses and gives a good feel for what makes them special. The website contains a discussion group, which I check frequently to keep up with what's going on in the golf world, and you can usually find out if there are going to be charity auctions for particular courses you might be interested in playing. In addition, occasionally there are postings about events being held that might be of interest.

I used blogging to assist in my quest. When I designed my blog, I created a list of all 100 courses I was trying to play, and each time I completed one I did a write-up about the course. People could come to my blog and see which courses I had already played and which ones I had yet to play. One of my secrets is I was invited to four private courses on my targeted play list by members who were tracking my progress and were proud to show off their home course. Whenever I received emails from people, I always Googled them to make sure they were legitimate and I wasn't likely to be slashed with a razor when I showed up. In all instances my hosts were true gentlemen who loved the game and were happy to share something with a fellow golf fanatic.

I chose to do my blog anonymously because I wanted to give honest reviews of courses and didn't want to offend any members if I didn't like their course. While pursuing the quest, I didn't want people to be deterred from extending me an invitation for fear of raising their club's profile, because many are publicity shy.

Over the last couple of years, blogs have proliferated, so you need something distinctive to grab people's attention. It is unlikely your blog will be as sardonic and wry as mine, but give it a go. Other golf bloggers worth noting are Graylynloomis.com, who spent four years golfing—and studying—at the University of St. Andrews and profiles courses and his experiences; and Golftripper.com, which is a good resource for courses located in the United States. While primarily a news aggregator, GeoffShackelford.com is also a must read, his comments are normally witty and to the point. My kids laugh and tell me blogs are for old people and I should use Twitter and Facebook, but I haven't met any members of top clubs yet on Facebook.

Another good resource is GHIN.com, which is run by the United States Golf Association and allows you to look up handicaps for anyone in the United States who has an official one. All you need to know is the person's name and home state, and, voilà, you can see what their handicap is; and more interesting for our purposes, you can see which club or clubs they belong to. In and of itself GHIN.com won't help you secure access; however, if you use it intelligently it can be a help. Let's say you meet an acquaintance through business or through social contacts and you suspect they are an avid golfer or member of a club you want to play. Simply look them up on GHIN.com and you will know. Hopefully, no one will take this advice and use it to stalk people or cold-call them, because that won't work.

One of the most interesting and sad stories related to GHIN.com is about former Merrill Lynch CEO Stanley O'Neal. Stan is an avid golfer and as his firm started to tank during the financial crisis, he apparently spent more time working on his handicap index than he did looking at the firm's balance sheet. An astute investor looked at what he was up to on GHIN.com, and saw that on key days during the crisis, Stan was out golfing rather than minding the shop. At the time, GHIN.com not only displayed your score and the date you played, but also where you played. Stan wasn't playing his local muni; in fact, he found time to play at Shinnecock Hills, at the private Vineyard Golf Club in Martha's Vineyard, and at the cloistered Golf Club of Purchase in New York. In the end, he was forced out of the firm, but the story illustrates how creative use of available information can be used for purposes other than they were originally intended. They have since changed the system so the name of the course played is not visible to the public.

An effective tool used by several people I know who are attempting to play top courses is an email distribution list. Sounds too simple, right? But it works. Periodically I receive emails from fellow golf fanatics who keep me and scores of others appraised of what courses they have played and what they still need to play. It has to be subtle to work; it can't be blatant requests to play. It helps to be entertaining and to combine it with a blog or other useful content, but I know several people have used this technique successfully. Part of the reason it works so well is because it is easy for someone who receives an email to forward it to a member of a course you want to play, to help you out.

Another interesting site is eBay. Sometimes a round of golf will go up for auction and you can set up searches similar to what I described with Google Alerts, so you will be notified when your keywords are matched, i.e., "Winged Foot Golf." I almost used this method to play the super-private Loch Lomond. Years ago, Loch Lomond hosted the Scottish Open Championship and one of the perks they had was to allow volunteers to play the course on a designated day after the tournament. One of the volunteers was attempting to auction off his slot and I was the eager top bidder before he removed the auction. Apparently the club found out he was doing this, were irritated, and made him take it down.

Another way to gather information about a club is to be used in emergency situations only. Since clubs in the United States operate as nonprofits they are required to file an annual form with the Internal Revenue Service titled "Form 990." Form 990s are public information and you can glean a tremendous amount of information about a club from them, including the size of its balance sheet, the amount of money it received the prior year in greens fees, its total membership dues, and its list of officers. In and of itself the information might not be particularly useful if you plan on cold-calling, but I have often been surprised at the names I have seen listed, and then established a plan to connect with them through a mutual contact or some other channel once I knew they played there.

Although technology has become a big help in trying to play at some of these famed clubs, in the pre-Internet, email, and blog era the task was slightly more complicated, although the pioneer highlighted in the closing story of this chapter didn't let it slow him down.

The Maiden Voyage

The first man to play the top 100 in the world was a forty-seven-year-old trial lawyer from New Orleans, who completed the task in a mere seven years. His name is Jim Wysocki, and he completed the journey in 1986, two years before the next person to do so. As mentioned, prior to various golf magazines' publishing top 100 lists, *Golf Magazine* published the "50 Greatest Golf Courses in the World." Wysocki also holds the distinction of being the first to finish this initial list, which he completed in 1982.

It took some time for me to find Jim's story because he did it in an era before all news stories were digitized and easily searchable. I had to research the old-fashioned way, looking at old newspapers from his hometown. Some interesting details struck me while reading about him in the *Times-Picayune*. A feature article says he somehow played three top 100 courses on three continents in one day, in London, New York, and Tokyo. Last time I checked, flying to Japan crosses the date line in the wrong direction, so I do not think he did it in one calendar day. It helps that Sunningdale, Garden City Golf Club, and Tokyo Golf Club are close to big city airports, and even if it wasn't on the same day, playing these three back-to-back-to-back or in a twenty-four-hour period is still quite a coup. As a frequent traveler, I would love to be able to receive one of the "good-conduct passes" he mentions to pass through customs quickly, so he could make his tee time in Japan. In today's era of air travel it would not happen.

Wysocki played out of Metairie Country Club and logged almost 300,000 miles on 105 separate flights en route to playing all the courses. His feat included a few courses no longer ranked by the magazines, including some in Indonesia, Morocco, and Sweden. An amateur pilot as well as a trial lawyer, he flew 12,000 of the miles in his own plane to play the courses. He accomplished the task before MapQuest and GPS technology and planned the trips using paper maps. Wysocki says the three best methods he used to gain access were to write letters to the courses, to ask for help from his clients, and to leverage his pro at Metairie Country Club. His favorite course was Pebble Beach.

It was as hard to play Augusta for him as it is for everyone else. The story of how he accessed Augusta was detailed in a *Times-Picayune* story on October 20, 1982. First, he asked the golf reporter for the *Times-Picayune* whether he could use his reporter's credentials after the tournament one year. He was rebuffed. "You can't imagine how many avenues I took and I was turned down," Wysocki said. As the reporter tells Jim's story, "He tried a former U.S. Attorney General and failed. A United States district judge and failed. A vice president of Lykes Brothers [the largest land owner in Florida], whose brother is a member and failed. He finally accomplished the impossible in a roundabout way. His wife Christina's sister introduced him to a couple who introduced him to their daughter whose husband is a doctor in Meridian, Mississippi. The doctor has a sister in Augusta who is married to someone in the trucking business. His trucks are insured by a company whose vice president is Phil Harison. Phil Harison's father is Montgomery Harison who helped found the club. It was that easy. Got the picture?"

To celebrate this groundbreaking accomplishment, the editors of *Golf Magazine* played with him on his final round at the Yale Golf Course and presented him with a hand-lettered, framed list of the courses acknowledging his achievement.

Jim tragically died in his early fifties in a Cessna plane crash in Louisiana in 1989, three short years after his accomplishment. In his honor, the James A. Wysocki Award is granted each year to students at Tulane who excel in trial advocacy. It's too bad Jim's life was cut short so early; he sounds like an interesting fellow and I would have enjoyed comparing notes with him.

CHAPTER THREE
Basic Techniques to Access Exclusive Golf Clubs

This chapter will share the basic methods you can use to play at some of the finest golf clubs. Aside from private courses overseas that allow unaccompanied guests to play, the best way to access private courses is to find a member. I was invited to only six of the top 100 courses I played by a member I knew directly. By networking, I was able to play twenty-four hard-to-access private courses in the United States. Finding a member is as simple and as difficult as making the right connections. I was lucky enough to work for a global investment firm when I was earnestly trying to play these courses, which benefited me because I knew a group of well-connected people in key cities across the country. When people heard the story of what I was trying to accomplish they were willing to help.

It is said that all seven billion people on earth are connected through only six degrees of separation. That is, by connecting to a friend or relative who taps into their network of friends and acquaintances, who does the same to their network, and continuing on down the line—after doing this six times—you can reach anyone. Perhaps, although it sounded to me like Jim Wysocki used more than six degrees to play Augusta. For my purposes, the deepest I had to go to gain access was to five degrees to play a very private course in Europe I will detail in a future chapter.

Networking and Making Connections

The easiest way to begin is to ask your own friends, relatives, or acquaintances to see if they know a member of Merion, if that is a course you want to play. To state the obvious, it is easier to find a member if you live in suburban Philadelphia—where the course is located—than if you live in Sheboygan, although Merion also has a large national membership. Acquaintances include business associates, advisors, vendors, or people you have met for the first time at cocktail parties or at golf outings. In my case, a friend knew a vendor who was a second-generation member of Merion and he hosted us. The other elite course located at the western end of Pennsylvania is Oakmont. To gain access to Oakmont I asked a colleague who lives in Pittsburgh, who had a client who was a member. Sometimes an invitation can happen within a month or two of asking; sometimes it takes years.

What won't work is cold-calling a member; 99 percent of the time it will fail. Put yourself in the member's place; you are called by someone you do not know asking to play. Why would you accommodate them? Members have to protect their membership and the last thing they want is someone who comes out with poor etiquette and embarrasses them, and as an unknown, you represent risk to them. Do you like getting cold calls at home at dinnertime? Unless you are unbalanced a bit, probably not. Think of asking to play without an introduction as the same thing; better to be introduced by an acquaintance or in some other fashion.

So, how can you improve your chances of networking and meeting a member? By improving your luck. Okay, you suspected the author was daft having undertaken such a quixotic journey to begin with. *What do you mean improving your luck? Isn't luck something you can't control?* I can hear you saying to yourself, by definition, luck is something brought on by chance. Well, to a degree luck is something you can't control, but as it relates to interacting with people, you can improve your luck quite a bit; partially it relates to your personality type and the way you behave.

The ideas are articulated in brilliant detail in *The Luck Factor* by Dr. Richard Wiseman. His advice first and foremost is to have a positive attitude and visualize events you want to happen; believe you are lucky. Gary Player is a prime illustration of this; I once asked Gary what books have had the most impact on him as a player and his answer was surprising: *The Power of Positive Thinking* by Dr. Norman Vincent Peale. Gary's belief, which is outlined in Peale's book, is you can will yourself to positivity, and he is right. The second piece of advice is be more outwardly focused if you want to meet the right people; being inwardly focused and laconic isn't going to help. As I pursued my quest I worked hard to improve my irritable and guarded personality to become more outwardly focused and open. A big part of the success I had in achieving my goal was that I was determined to figure out a way to eventually play even the difficult-to-access courses, and I believed I would. As Henry Ford famously said, "If you think you can do a thing or think you can't do a thing, you're right."

A good example to illustrate the idea is plane travel. My natural inclination when traveling is to be left alone. A chatty seatmate would be met with one-word answers or with me sending signals I wasn't interested in a chat. Bad idea. The more people you meet and the more stories you hear, the more connections you will make. Case in point: I was flying from Florida back to New York one summer night and our plane hit strong thunderstorms and started bouncing around. The elderly gentleman next to me was nervous and started to talk to me. Our initial banter about hoping we stay aloft soon turned to golf (doesn't every conversation?). He was a retired vice-chairman of a money-center bank, a member of Seminole, and was once on the waiting list to become a member of Augusta. Augusta has a membership that is more advanced in age than your average club and he was never invited to join because all his sponsors died before he could be accepted. We talked for an hour about golf and our favorite courses, and we had some mutual acquaintances. If I had kept to myself I never would have met him or heard his stories. I ended up playing Seminole through someone else, but it does illustrate that you never know who you are talking to. While talking to strangers on a plane works well seated in coach, it works even better if you are upgraded to first-class.

The more people you know, the more connections you develop, the better your chances of securing the round of golf you want. My advice would be to play in member-guest and charity golf outings and talk to people you haven't met before, and it will improve your luck. Be open to new experiences, go to events you normally wouldn't go to, talk to people you typically do not, and you will be surprised at how it helps improve your opportunities for success. Of course, you are going to run into your fair share of blowhards, fools, and insufferable people along the way, but that's part of the fun.

Networking is certainly easier if you are a member of a top golf club. Of the twenty-five people that have completed playing the top 100 courses in the world, several are members of exclusive clubs, such as the Olympic Club, Riviera, the Country Club at Brookline, the Royal & Ancient Golf Club of St. Andrews, and Baltusrol. The reason it helps is because the top clubs often offer reciprocity to members of other top clubs and you tend to meet members with good connections. The task of finding members was somewhat harder for me because I am not a member of one of these clubs.

While most of the people I interacted with on my journey were more than happy to help, some people guard their contacts extra closely, especially if they have a legitimate way onto Augusta or know a member of Cypress Point. One of the most jealously guarded introductions of all is to a Japanese businessman who is a networking ninja and has a bulging Rolodex of contacts at all the top private clubs there.

Who Are These Guys?

So, who are members of these illustrious clubs? Ultimately, I have no clue, but I can offer some generalizations based on my experiences. Maybe because I am in the industry I have a jaded view, but many of the people I played with were in the financial world. There are a lot of Wall Street types that belong to clubs, including people who work at banks, investment firms, mutual fund companies, insurance companies, private equity firms, hedge funds, and other related firms. This is particularly true for courses around New York City. Similarly, "the City," as the financial industry is known in the United Kingdom, is well represented among private clubs around London.

Following this theme, it is logical to look at what company or industry is dominant in a particular city as a starting point. Proctor and Gamble is based in Cincinnati, home of the Seth Raynor designed Camargo, so it follows that executives of P & G would be good connections and possible members. Similarly, Anheuser-Busch executives would have connections to access courses in St. Louis. The same would be true of

Coca-Cola in the Atlanta area, although this is not always the case. You would think the San Francisco Golf Club would have a large number of technology executives as members but it does not. In fact, it prides itself on being more "old" money than new, and has admitted few of the dot-com coterie as members.

Beyond a high concentration of members from the financial world, I can tell you the other types of people I was actually hosted by as an indicator of membership. Two were doctors, three were lawyers, many were owners of their own businesses, two were serial entrepreneurs, a half-dozen were corporate executives, and one clipped coupons—not the type you use in the supermarket—and walked to his mailbox to pick up his paycheck. My experience of hosts is borne out if you look at the occupations of those that have completed playing the top 100 in the world. More than 25 percent were in the financial services industry, an equal number were business owners, one was a strategy consultant, one was an attorney, and the rest were corporate executives.

My experiences tell me members of the most exclusive clubs do not normally volunteer telling you they are members. Unlike people who attend Harvard, who have a tendency to work into the conversation within five minutes of meeting you that they are graduates, in the golf world, when meeting people for the first time, they do not normally stick out their hand and say, "Hey John, nice to meet you, I'm a member of Maidstone." You can tell when someone is golf obsessed and plays at lot and can pick up subtle hints. If in doubt, you could look on GHIN.com to see where they play.

Geography matters; eight of those that have completed the world's best live in California, four in the New York area, and three are from the golf-rich state of Ohio. My journey was clearly aided by the firm I worked for and I had geography on my side. Thirteen of the top 100 courses are within a three-hour drive of my home or office in Midtown Manhattan, and another dozen are within a short plane ride. It helped that in my role I had to travel extensively throughout the United States, so if I was going to be in Denver anyway, why not bring my clubs along and play Cherry Hills?

Most clubs typically have 300–400 members, some of the more elite courses have less. Chicago Golf Club has only about 125, the Valley Club of Montecito only 225, Seminole 350, Garden City and Augusta, around 300, and Yeamans Hall and Cypress Point, 250 each; although Cypress Point's local members number only about seventy-five. Some clubs have multiple classes of memberships, so Merion will have a small number of local members, around 300, but a larger national membership for people living around the country who do not come and play often. The same for Pine Valley, which has fifty or so overseas members, about 250 resident members, and 425 nonresident members. Clubs such as Baltusrol and Winged Foot, with two golf courses, would have a larger membership.

Every club has its own philosophy regarding membership. Some have selective memberships and are concentrated with CEOs and other elite. This is clearly true of Augusta but also of Loch Lomond, Seminole, and Chicago Golf. Others have a more national membership and are used as "retreats," such as the Honors Course in Tennessee or Ocean Forest in Georgia. The Tom Fazio–designed Wade Hampton club near Asheville, North Carolina, is such a tough place to be invited to—it was one of the last courses I played—because in order to be a member you need to own a home on the property. The predominant characteristic Pine Valley members have in common is they are low-handicapped golfers.

You will have hit the jackpot it you can find a member who belongs to multiple clubs. There are a couple of well-known globetrotters who are members of close to a dozen clubs, and I won't reveal their names because it is bad form to do so. A good example from the last generation was Sir Peter Allen, who served as chairman of Britain's Imperial Chemical Industries. He was a member of the Royal & Ancient Golf Club of St. Andrews, Rye, Royal St. George's, the Royal Cinque Ports, and the Oxford & Cambridge Golfing Society. And these were only his clubs in the United Kingdom. He was also a member of Pine Valley and was Augusta's first non-American member.

Remember Your Manners

Okay, so you meet a member of a club you want to play, how do you approach the ask? My advice is to go slowly and be patient. Less is more when it comes to asking. Hopefully you have done your homework and know something about the course or club, so you can say you love Tillinghast courses and you've always wanted to play there. Be subtle and first develop a relationship. I've found a direct ask usually isn't the best approach, as counterintuitive as that seems; remember the basic manners your mother taught you. As bad as it is to ask straightaway in America, it is completely out of the cultural norm in Great Britain to be aggressive and ask to play up front; it's the equivalent of asking someone what their bank balance is upon first meeting them.

One unwritten rule is you cannot ask a member of Augusta for an invitation to play because it is an automatic "no." At almost any other course in the world it is fine to politely ask a member at the right time to play, but at Augusta it will not work. Knowing this rule, on the handful of occasions I met Augusta members through my job I would dance around the subject, work golf into the conversation, and do everything I could short of asking, but it didn't work. It is a hard club to gain access to.

My final piece of advice is emphasized in *The Luck Factor*, which is, after you've planted a few seeds, relax. Sometimes when you stop pressing for a goal and sit back, things fall into place without any effort. When I began my journey I didn't know anything about St. George's, a classic Stanley Thompson–designed course, including where Etobicoke, Ontario, is. My favorite flower is the impatient and my favorite department in the hospital is the "In Patient" department. In other words, patience has never been one of my strong suits. As I mentioned in the technology chapter, sometimes things happen out of the blue when you are not pressing. I was invited to play by a blog reader who was a member and a real gentleman, and we remain friends to this day.

Return to Sender

Just to reinforce how difficult Augusta is to play, I even had a friend who knew a member write them an old-fashioned letter you send through the mail, telling him about my journey and asking on my behalf. We never heard a word. Perhaps the postal service lost the letter in transit? More likely than not Augusta members receive more than their fair share of letters like this and it is easier to ignore them than to respond.

I guess I shouldn't be surprised, though, because I experience the same thing. It never ceases to amaze me some of the email traffic I receive by having a blog that highlights courses I have played. Because the elusive Cypress Point—the number two ranked course in the world—doesn't have its own website people assume I would be a good proxy to help them book a tee time. One of the best requests I received was from an "ultra-luxury travel" company asking for a reservation, "We have a client who would like to play Cypress Point Golf Club during the weekend of May 23 and 24. My client is able to pay a fee for the privilege. Would you be able to arrange to play Cypress Point? If not, can you suggest someone else who I can contact?" I am always tempted to reply back. "Absolutely, this should be no problem, how is 10:30 a.m. on Saturday morning?" but I let them go without reply.

Etiquette

Assuming you are invited to play, there are some basic rules to follow since proper etiquette is important in the game of golf generally, and is especially important at private clubs. Do your research, understand the club's history, and know something about them—for example, at some courses the rules require you to wear a jacket and tie. The most famous course in the United States where you are required to wear a jacket is Garden City Golf Club—known as "The Men's" or "Garden City Men's"—on Long Island. It doesn't matter what else you have on, but you must have a suit jacket on to enter. I have seen men walk in with shorts, sneakers, and a suit jacket, which is fine, but the etiquette must be followed. Once inside The Men's it is acceptable to take off your jacket. Another example where you must wear a jacket is at Oakmont in Pittsburgh, where one is required for dinner. In the United Kingdom many clubs require you to wear at least a jacket, and sometimes a jacket and tie to sit in the member's dining room. A club with one of the most stringent rules in the United Kingdom is the Honourable Company of Edinburgh Golfers, more commonly known as Muirfield. To enter Muirfield, you must be wearing your jacket and a tie. As the club that helped establish many of the game's rules and traditions, who are you to argue with their rules? It is rather civilized.

Other commonsense tips: Do not bring your cell phone, BlackBerry, or other devices that make noise. Golf clubs are refuges from the demands of daily life and most clubs restrict their use; leave them at home or in the car. Bring sufficient money to tip the appropriate people in the club, including the locker room attendant and the caddies. Be sure to research or ask beforehand on the policies of the club; some have strict no-tipping rules, others want you to tip; if in doubt, ask the member. Of course, offer to pay for your round, although I found in many instances the member will refuse because they are gracious hosts. Pay for your own caddie and for your host's. After the round, send your host a thank-you note or email.

Some courses require you to play with the member and allow no unaccompanied guests. I experienced this firsthand at Seminole. A playing partner and I played with a local physician, and he told us when we met that he was on call, and if there was an emergency and he had to leave, we had to as well. Since no phones are allowed on the course, while we were on the 13th tee an assistant pro came driving out in a golf cart with an urgent call for the doctor. My playing partner and I looked at each other in despair. He spoke with the patient in need and luckily for us gave her the "Take two aspirin and call me in the morning" advice, and we played on.

A handful of clubs outside the United States require a minimum handicap in order for you to play. In Australia, Royal Melbourne requires your handicap to be below twenty-eight for men. While it is not the custom in the United States to impose handicap limits, the notable exception is Bethpage Black on Long Island, where they suggest only "low-handicap" golfers play, although they do not impose a numerical limit.

Some clubs, although not many, require you to wear long pants. The Los Angeles Country Club is one of the few in the United States where you cannot wear shorts. Augusta National is another. Several in the United Kingdom are the same, although some will let you play in shorts if you have on long socks. Golfing in Japan requires long pants, although there are so many nuances and rituals about playing there that I cover them in full detail in a chapter dedicated to the subject. Most important of all, play fast. Nobody likes slow play and private clubs generally move at a good pace. Most golf clubs in the United Kingdom expect you to be around the course in three and a half hours.

If you do not have good connections and are still trying to find a way to play at an exclusive course, there are many other techniques that might work, which I outline below. The remainder of this chapter is dedicated to these basic techniques. Later in the book I will outline some advanced ways I was able to secure invitations to courses that are more difficult.

Charity Events and Fund-raisers

One of the simplest ways to access exclusive golf courses is to donate money. Giving back to the community has always been a hallmark of the game. The US PGA Tour has given a cumulative two billion dollars to charities. Member clubs and individual members are also philanthropically oriented and host charity outings. The list of courses in the United States that host charity outings is a who's who of US Open venues and includes Shinnecock Hills, Baltusrol, Oakmont, Winged Foot, and Oak Hill. The easiest way to find them was discussed in the technology chapter: use Google or subscribe to one of the services mentioned. Doing this will highlight the big events; that is, days where the entire course is dedicated to the outing, most typically on Mondays, when member play is normally restricted. While bidding on a charity auction offers you a way onto a course you might not otherwise be able to network into through a member, it is not inexpensive. If you pay $500 per golfer you've done well; often it is more than $1,000 a golfer for the most sought-after courses. If you have the money, it's worth doing since you are supporting a good cause. Similarly, you do not have to participate in a big outing; many charity events or fund-raisers have silent auctions, where you can bid on a threesome or foursome at a desirable course. This is a more intimate experience than a larger outing and you will meet a member and enjoy more of the overall club experience. It's hard to argue your money is not being well spent giving back to the community, and you receive a tax deduction.

Tiger Woods Charity Playoffs

An interesting method to play at some of the most storied clubs is through the Tiger Woods Charity Playoffs, which he sponsors to raise money. The 2014 version of the program included playing at venues such as the Myopia Hunt Club near Boston, Merion, and the Congressional Country Club in Maryland. To enter, you play in

Myopia Hunt Club, South Hamilton, Massachusetts, 9th hole.

two-person teams and the fee is $500 per player, which includes the round of golf, access to the clubhouse, the locker room, and lunch. In addition to the entry fee, each team is required to give an additional $2,000 ($1,000 per player) in donations, with the money going toward helping underserved children through the Tiger Woods Foundation or Kids on the Hill charity.

Play in a Pro-Am

A subset of the charity technique is to participate in a pro-am, which also raises money for charity. Playing in a pro-am for tour events even works at such world-class courses as Colonial or Riviera in Los Angeles. It is a good way to play the course if you can swing it—plus, you have the added benefit of playing with a tour pro and meeting other golfers. Often times, the slots at pro-ams are controlled by the sponsoring organization. In the case of Riviera, the tournament is called the Northern Trust Open and Northern Trust would control a majority of the pro-am invitations. Likewise, tee times at the Crown Plaza Invitational at Colonial would be allotted to the sponsoring hotel group. Do research on the sponsors and go to tournament websites and you can see whether this is a feasible approach for you or not. If you are worried you do not have the game for a pro-am, relax; you play the member tees, not the pro tees, and their caddie will yell "fore" when you launch one into the gallery.

Leverage Your Club Professional

Club professionals in the United States are members of the PGA of America. As you saw from Jim Wysocki's success, your club pro can sometimes be helpful in getting you access to a course you want to play. If you are a member of a desirable course, your pro has more influence than most and can book you a tee time on a course you want. Even if you are not a member of one of the top courses, your pro may have good connections depending on their tenure. It's worth a try. I was able to get onto some US Open venues, including Southern Hills in Oklahoma, through a club pro. There are multiple classes of PGA professionals and a seniority system; the more senior your pro, the better their connections. To give some stunningly obvious examples, the head pro at Oakmont in the summer serves as the head pro at Seminole in the winter. It would be hard to imagine another pro turning down a request to play from Bob Ford. Or, the pro at Maidstone on Long Island spends his winters at the exclusive Calusa Pines in Naples. Membership has its privileges indeed. If you go this route, flexibility is key. Since they are doing you a favor, give them multiple dates when you can play and a story to tell. If you play a course this way, make sure you thank the pro of the course you are visiting and buy something in the pro shop to support them.

Join a Golfing Society

Another method to access courses is to join a golfing society, which costs a couple of hundred dollars. A golfing society is a group of like-minded people who have an affin-

Fishers Island, New York, Biarritz, 5th hole.

ity for a particular golf course architect and periodically gather to play the architect's courses. One of the most desirable is the Seth Raynor Society. Among others courses, Raynor was the designer of Fox Chapel in Pittsburgh, Camargo in Cincinnati, Shoreacres near Chicago, Yeamans Hall in Charleston, and Fishers Island in New York. It is a list of dream courses. Raynor had an eye for designing appealing courses that are among the game's best, and it is not surprising he has a large following of fans. A recent outing of the society was held at a Raynor course in Minnesota and had a participation fee of $250. In addition to getting to play a fabulous course, you will meet other golf aficionados who share an interest in golf course architecture, which can only help you. Raynor often worked with Charles Blair Macdonald and Charles Banks. Macdonald needs no further introduction and Banks created some fantastic courses, such as Forsgate in New Jersey and Whippoorwill in New York. The Raynor Society is open to members or employees of clubs designed by any of these three architects, although they sometimes let in members who are not.

Whippoorwill Club, Armonk, New York, 4th hole.

In addition to the Raynor Society, there is the Donald Ross Society, which hosts a number of events at Ross courses around the country. There are societies for the five-time Open Champion and designer James Braid; there is an A. W. Tillinghast Association, an association for H. S. Colt, and a society for one of my favorite architects, the iconoclastic Englishman Tom Simpson. A Canadian-based golf society is for members that appreciate the thick-mustached, cigar-smoking, fedora hat–wearing architect of many of Canada's premier golf courses; a man who had an affinity for wearing three-piece suits with a watch-chain hanging down, and for fifteen-ounce steaks: Stanley Thompson.

Become a Golf Course Rater

When you are a rater for a golf magazine many courses will allow you to come and play so you can rate their course. *Golf Magazine* has the most stringent criteria to become a rater and they have to pick you; you can't apply. You can ask *Golf Digest* to be a rater if you are a low handicapper, or *Golfweek,* if you travel frequently, have knowledge of courses, and follow their rules. I was a rater with them for a time and found the revered courses discourage raters. Everyone knows they are great and they do not need more affirmation from the ratings panels. You are discouraged from trying to use your rating credentials to try to access the pantheon of courses, and even risk being fired as a rater if you do so.

George Peper wrote an article in *Links Magazine* in 2006 where he cited comments from some of the top courses after he launched a ranking of golf courses as editor of *Golf Magazine.* He quotes Pine Valley president Ernie Ransom as saying, "You've done our club a tremendous disservice, everyone wants to play here now and 99 percent of the requests can't be granted." Similarly, Fishers Island's position is succinct: "We do not wish our course to be ranked, visited or for that matter known. Please convey that to your panelists." Be warned, it is hard to receive permission to play, and you won't be the first person to ignore the advice and try it anyway. I know a *Golf Magazine* rater who attended a meeting of raters at Baltusrol; the pro gave a talk and said they receive several hundred requests a year to play from raters and they politely tell them they can't accommodate them without a member.

Gaining access as a rater does tend to work for newer courses eager to break into the rankings. Course owners, particularly Donald Trump, love to have their courses ranked, so your best bet would be trying to access any course with his name on it, if you so desire. Similarly, other undiscovered courses most people have never heard of are happy to welcome raters and often they will not charge you for playing. One of the real benefits of being a rater is meeting other raters at periodic events they hold and there are valuable connections to be made.

Ask a Course Owner

For newer courses sometimes it works to ask the owner, especially if they are of the Man in Full or benevolent-dictator type. I know one of my fellow questers used this technique to access some exclusive courses; and he didn't play as an unaccompanied guest, the master of the universe played with him.

Call the Course and Ask

In the United States there are two schools of thought regarding unaccompanied guests. One is that they are welcomed by clubs since they bring in revenue. The other is that unless you are invited by a member you aren't welcome. In my experience almost all clubs follow the latter, since they do not want to engage in activities

The Alister MacKenzie–designed Crystal Downs in Michigan.

that are perceived as solely for the purpose of raising revenue, lest they jeopardize their tax-exempt status.

While this technique doesn't work often, there can be exceptions. It is unlikely to work for courses near big cities or those in demand to be played. It works on courses that are respected but a bit off the beaten track. Flexibility is the key; you have to be able to play off-week or off-season but if done in the correct manner with the proper respect, it works. It worked for me on a course in Michigan ranked within the top twenty-five in the world designed by Alister MacKenzie: Crystal Downs, which I played on a weekday in late October.

Get a "Peg" Board

As I mentioned, a dear friend who shot 78 the first time he played Royal Melbourne's West course gave me a wooden board that lists top golf courses. I hung the board in my office at work and it was a natural conversation piece. It completely changes the dynamic of having to be a golf whore. People look at it and ask what it is; most think it's neat and scan down the list of courses. Typically, they will say, "Oh, I know a member at Oakland Hills, I should introduce you." My experience is you do not have to ask with the peg board up, people volunteer to help. The boards are sold through Golf Links to the Past, located in Pebble Beach, and are available for sale on their website.

One of the ultimate coups in my quest was the way I played the number one ranked course in the world, which I am fortunate to live an hour from. One day I was sitting in my office and a colleague came in and we started talking. He had been in my office countless times before and had seen my peg board but never said anything. In an utter act of goodwill and kindness, he said out of the blue, "Hey John, we should go out and play Pine Valley; are you interested?" I didn't even know he was a member.

I was speechless for a good thirty seconds as it registered. When I told him yes, he said, "Great, how does Sunday look?" Putting aside that I would have to skip going to church, my son's soccer game, and my wedding anniversary (just kidding on the last point, but that would be a tough call), I said, "Sunday looks open," to which he replied, "As long as the weather holds up, let's do it." For the next five days I checked the weather online every half hour. One of my friends who was jealous I was playing was hoping there would be a nor'easter on the appointed day, but the weather was ideal—a crisp fall day with a temperature of seventy-three degrees and low humidity. The Weather Channel's "golf index" indicator tells the whole story, it was: "10 out of 10 (Excellent)."

On the morning of my round, I put on my finest dress slacks and best golf shirt; no fraying khakis at Pine Valley. I prepared my car, filled it with gas, and checked the tire pressure, the oil, and the wiper fluid. If you haven't figured it out, I'm a little compulsive, but nothing was going to stop me from having a flawless day. I drove down the New Jersey Turnpike at fifty-five miles per hour, which is difficult to do since the average car and truck

Pine Valley, New Jersey, a stand-alone golf course and township.

is going over seventy miles per hour. I was a little-old-lady out for my Sunday drive. I did not need to be pulled over by a state trooper on my way to Pine Valley so I was taking no chances at all. I also brought plenty of cash, because the pro shop didn't take credit cards at the time (it does now) and I wanted to buy a large quantity of logoed merchandise.

New Jersey is a most unusual state in many ways, especially when it comes to something called local-rule. Even though it is one of the smallest states, it has over 550 separate municipalities or governing bodies. Aside from being a revered golf course, Pine Valley is its own stand-alone municipality, which consists of only the golf course and a few houses owned by members. Under New Jersey law every municipality has to have a town hall, a school district, et cetera, in order to be able to govern itself. Pine Valley has each of these and its own stand-alone police force as well. It is set up this way so it can keep complete control over its affairs without anybody poking into its business.

Pine Valley's location—similar to the presidential retreat at Camp David—isn't exactly unknown, you just have go out of your way to find it. Located in an ordinary middle-class New Jersey suburb, the area surrounding the course is not grand and does not hint at the greatness that exists behind the fence separating this unrivaled place from the rest of the world. To get to Pine Valley you drive to the tiny Clementon Amusement Park, which saw its best days long ago but still functions seasonally. Behind the amusement park, down a two-lane road, on the other side of a set of railroad tracks is the Pine Valley Administration building. This Lilliputian building contains the entire infrastructure for the town of Pine Valley, population twenty, which includes the municipal court, police headquarters, and town hall.

I drove over the railroad tracks, through the fence, and approached the guardhouse. My name was on the clipboard, I had no food sticking out of my teeth, and my fly was zipped, so I was waved in. I had re-read *Zen Golf* in anticipation of playing and tried to settle myself down a little because it is such a peerless place: remember to breathe, meditate, and enter the zone. The clubhouse is modest and understated and has few trappings, because it is about golf only. It would do the officials at the USGA and PGA a world of good to visit Pine Valley every so often as a refresher in what makes golf great. It is not about having high rough or lots of water, it is about the strategic nature of the course and having to use your head to play well.

The course is, no doubt about it, one of the best in the world, and the club and the township an exclusive enclave. When playing at Pine Valley you are away from the world and communing with nature. The routing of the course is the best in the world; it is so diverse and well thought-out. To give you a sense of how much attention they pay to course conditioning, after they cut the fairways, they take a rope and pull it across them to remove excess clippings so they are pristine. The sandy waste areas off the fairway are to be avoided because they are true hazards. There are no rakes in any of the sand and being in them is a quick way to run up a big number. It is certainly one of the most visually intimidating courses in the world. Every tee shot requires a forced carry over the menacing sandy waste areas. Unwavering pinpoint accuracy is required

Pine Valley, 9th hole.

to score well at Pine Valley. If you are long and accurate off the tee, the fairways are lush and generous, setting you up to score well; if you have the misfortune of slicing or pulling your tee shot, or—heaven forbid—hitting it short of the fairways, Pine Valley will torture you. Assuming you hit the fairways, the key to scoring is holding the perfectly conditioned and lightning fast greens (easier said than done) and having a deft touch while putting.

We stopped for lunch after our morning round and then played again. The entire experience had an out-of-body feeling for me and luckily I played a bit better than my handicap. By the end of the day I was never more physically and mentally drained in all my life. After I drove home I opened a bottle of Irish whiskey I had been saving for a special occasion, a twenty-five-year-old Bushmills Millennium Malt, bottled in the year 2000, and sipped it neat, accompanied by a Bolivar No. 2. I passed out on my back deck a happy man. Although I travel frequently and pride myself on being home so I can attend all my kids' sporting events, I had to make an exception and missed my son's game, which he has forgiven me for.

As an illustration of how revered Pine Valley is in the world of golf, consider the story Jack Nicklaus tells in his biography *My Story*. He was on his honeymoon and driving from New York to Atlantic City, which isn't far from the course. He arrived at the course unannounced and asked if he could play. They accommodated him but at the time Pine Valley didn't allow women on the property, so his wife, Barbara, stayed outside the fence, driving around, trying to spy him occasionally around the perimeter.

Pine Valley is the true north of a pure golfing experience and every golfer should try to visit at least once, even if you can't play the course. Each September the club hosts the Crump Cup, their club championship and a private tournament, and they allow spectators to come and watch on the final Sunday. After parking at the nearby amusement park, yellow buses—wholly appropriate because you feel like a child who is agog on your way to the first day of school—shuttle you over to the course. Spectators are allowed unrestricted access (for a twenty-dollar parking fee) to the grounds without any ropes up, although you are not allowed in the pro shop or clubhouse. It is worth attending so you can see the property and the impressive routing.

CHAPTER FOUR

The Easy Courses to Play and Leveraging Resorts and Hotels

S ome of the best courses in the world are available to play without too much fuss and I will detail them in this chapter. Playing the courses highlighted here is often a credible substitute in cases where you can't play the private club of a similar ilk. To some degree Pebble Beach is a poor man's Cypress Point—poor being a relative term; Sea Island is a poor man's way to play Ocean Forest, and the same with Old Macdonald or the Mid Ocean Club if you can't play the National Golf Links. Since the courses and resorts in the United States are well-known I will cover them quickly and focus on those that have some unique twist. Do not read too much into my opinion of a course if I fail to elaborate on it, since I am focusing on the trickier ones. One of the best techniques you can use to play great golf, as you will see below, is to stay at the right hotel. The obvious and not-so-obvious courses where you can do so are covered in this chapter.

Let's begin with resort golf and Pebble Beach, which is a must-visit. I love Pebble Beach and it is a rewarding place to play, although it does have a half-dozen average holes. The reason Pebble Beach is ultimately so amazing, though, is because the holes that are good are *so* good they end up overcompensating for the weaker holes. Dip into your savings and stay at the Lodge; it's worth the splurge, and putting off your retirement won't kill you. A kilt-wearing bagpiper comes out to play as the sun sets at the Lodge—his backdrop is Monterey Bay with dolphins jumping in the distant water, and it sends the spirits soaring, particularly with a cocktail in hand and with the fire pit burning. Pace of play is an issue at Pebble Beach because of the crowds, so be prepared for either a slow round or a round where a ranger pushes you on every hole, or both.

Nearby Spyglass Hill is rewarding to play; it has what are probably the best five opening holes in the world, that play from the top of a hill sweeping down to the water. Farther up the West Coast, the Bandon Dunes resort is pure golf at its finest; it is a walking only facility, with a fabulous caddie program. Its basic, comfortable lodges are a close approximation to the experience of staying overnight at a private club. In addition, you can have endless debates with your playing partners about what you think the better course is; my preference is for the original Bandon Dunes course designed by Scotsman David McLay Kidd.

A pair of Pete Dye courses in South Carolina should also be on your short list, starting with the Ocean Course at Kiawah; and take out a second mortgage so you can stay at their luxury resort, the Sanctuary. Harbour Town is worth visiting on the same trip, since it was one of Dye's earliest designs and features narrow fairways and small greens and highlights his imaginative use of railroad ties.

Pinehurst is the spiritual home of golf in the United States, and everyone should play the Donald Ross gem of No. 2 and stay at one of the three in-town properties: the Carolina Hotel, the Holly Inn, or the Pine Crest Inn; it is one of the top twenty-five golf courses in the world, and walking the fairways at dawn or dusk with the smell of pine in the air and the sound of church bells ringing softly in the village is magical. The Homestead Resort in Virginia is golf with Southern hospitality and pays homage to Sam Snead, who served as the professional there for a long time. It has an interesting William Flynn mountain course, designed in 1923. West Virginia's Greenbrier has a worthy Charles Blair Macdonald design and a hotel that is a National Historic Landmark; there is no mistaking that you have entered Dixie with buttered grits and sausage gravy on the breakfast menu. Whistling Straits and the Kohler Resort are easy to stay at and play, although the season is short in Wisconsin. I'm not the biggest fan of the

Stadium course at TPC Sawgrass; it has one gimmicky—albeit good—made-for-television hole, the 17th, but otherwise the Bermuda grass is too thick, there is too much water, and it has too many mediocre holes. A course in Florida that is a pleasant surprise is the Pine Barrens course at World Woods, which was ranked in the top 100 in the world when I played it but has subsequently dropped off the rankings. It was designed by Tom Fazio with Pine Valley in mind and has more similarities to the original than I thought it would, especially the untamed waste areas; it's cheap to play, making it a poor man's Pine Valley, which is not entirely coincidental since Fazio designed Pine Valley's short course. Both courses at the Streamsong Resort are excellent. The winning formula used at both the Bandon resort and the Barnbougle resort in Tasmania works here, which is the combination of two world-class courses designed by today's in-vogue designers: Streamsong features a Tom Doak course, the Blue, and a Coore & Crenshaw course, the Red.

Streamsong Resort, Florida, 7th hole, Blue Course.

The Sea Island Resort's hotels in Georgia have more five-star ratings than the Pentagon has five-star generals. The properties cost so much to build that the original owners filed for bankruptcy, but it is now operating in high style and will lighten your wallet. I prefer the Lodge to the Cloisters, although both are first-class. Play the Seaside course, a Colt & Alison design that Bobby Jones said had some of the best holes he had seen; it also has an uncommon attribute among golf courses, one it shares with Merion—it has red wicker baskets instead of pin flags.

The Caribbean, Atlantic, Mexico, and Canada

The Jack Nicklaus–designed Ocean Course at Cabo del Sol in Mexico can be played easily by booking a tee time online, and they have a resort hotel associated with the club. The Mid Ocean Club, a Charles Blair Macdonald–designed course in Bermuda is a private club, but non-members can play it on Mondays, Wednesdays, and Fridays if staying at the club's hotel. Staying at Sandy Lane in Barbados, where Tiger held his wedding, provides you access to the Fazio-designed Green Monkey.

Casa de Campo (Teeth of the Dog) is a Pete Dye course located in the Dominican Republic, and is unique in that it has some holes that you play while essentially standing at sea level. Many holes at famous courses are near or above the water; Casa de Campo differs from them because you are right at sea level. At Pebble Beach or Turnberry, for example, you are well up above the water. While playing Casa de Campo's 7th hole, the crystal-clear Caribbean water crashes immediately behind you, to the side of you, and ahead of you, on the same level you are standing. You can stay at the resort, which is convenient, but make sure you fly from the nearby airport in La Romana, which I did not, so you can learn from my moronic mistake. It is only ten minutes from the course, rather than the ninety-minute ride I endured.

When I visited, I had a 7 a.m. flight out of Santo Domingo on my day of departure. Given the distance the resort is from the airport, I arranged a taxi pickup at 3:30 a.m. so that I could arrive with enough time to clear the chaotic security lines. After passing through one of the little towns en route, we were driving in near total darkness when the driver began to slow. I didn't see the soldiers until we almost hit one of them, but there was a troop carrier off to the side of the road and the soldiers were checking cars driving by, although I didn't see any other cars. They were dressed in green and brown camouflage uniforms and there were no streetlights or other signs of civilization. The clock in the minivan was precisely 4 a.m., I remember this for a certainty because I was in a panic. The driver had a heated discussion in Spanish with one of the soldiers for an eternal two minutes. Given the language barrier I was unable to comprehend what it was about, although he said *dinero* after we pulled away. Perhaps an unofficial toll plaza set up by some enterprising soldiers? Whatever it was, it was at times such as this I questioned whether trying to play all these courses was a sane venture.

In addition to some world-class private courses, Canada has some of the best public golf available. Highlands Links in Nova Scotia, designed by Stanley Thompson, is set in the 600-acre Cape Breton National Park and takes full advantage of it. Sometimes when playing a course ranked among the top in the world it is a big disappointment, and, I think to myself, why is it so highly regarded? This was not the case at Highlands—it is what a top course should be: something special. The dramatic scenery in all directions is complemented by challenging golf holes and a varied routing, making it a standout. Categorizing Highlands Links is difficult because it combines some elements that typically do not go together, although it is best summed up by Thompson himself, who called it a "mountain and ocean course." The course is in a remote location but the Keltic Lodge Resort nearby is convenient when playing there. The other reason to go to Nova Scotia is to visit Cabot Links, brainchild of Canadian entrepreneur Ben Cowan-Dewar. The golf course was designed by fellow Canadian Rod Whitman, whose design philosophy is "strategic design coupled with great contour." His mentors were some of the best in the business, Bill Coore and Pete Dye. Cabot Links is located in the old coal-mining town of Inverness, a classic company town whose early housing, built at the turn of the last century, still stands today. A true links layout, Cabot is made for walking, and is the type of course where you want to walk back to the first tee after you walk off the final green. The new Cabot Cliffs course, situated on higher seaside land on a nearby bluff, built by the Coore & Crenshaw team, has made visiting Nova Scotia more often a must for the serious golfer. Both courses are accessible flying through the maritime city of Halifax, and you have the added benefit of driving the picturesque

Cabot Trail when doing so. And lobster is so ubiquitous there that you can eat it to your heart's content.

Las Vegas

One of the more prominent examples of using a hotel to gain access to a golf course is Shadow Creek in Las Vegas. The only way to play the course is to stay at an MGM resort in the city and pay a pricey greens fee. When I played it was $500. They do not take tee times without staying at the hotel, and it has been reported they have turned down former President George W. Bush and Canada's prime minister because neither were staying at an MGM resort.

Shadow Creek was conceived and financed by Steve Wynn, a hotel and casino magnate who spent a mammoth $40 million on it. He hired Tom Fazio to design the course and they took a 360-acre expanse of desert, moved 2.8 million cubic yards of earth, and planted 21,000 mature pine trees. In one of the more notable aspects of playing a top course, you are driven there in a stretch limousine.

The clubhouse is a decidedly understated affair, and surprisingly, given the city it is in, Shadow Creek is not about glitz. Since the temperature is normally around 100 degrees at midday, you are given a golf cart, but we didn't use ours, since, for me golf is a walking game. Instead, our caddie used it to drive the bags around so he didn't have to carry them. Forget everything you've heard about it not being that hot: you know the expression, "it's a dry heat." Not when I was there. Shadow Creek is more akin to playing in the Carolina Pines because of all the trees they have planted, and it has humidity, which is created by all the moisture coming out of the ground. My advice is to not wear your best shirt when playing Shadow Creek on a sunny day. I drank eight bottles of water, and although I didn't feel myself perspiring, the salt stains left on my shirt permanently ruined it. The locker room is allegedly modeled after Seminole's, but it felt a bit forced to me, especially putting famous people's names on lockers, which they could have done without. Nevertheless, playing Shadow Creek was a memorable day's golf. Having such a lush environment in the desert is a paradox and time will tell whether the whole enterprise is sustainable or a fool's errand.

Before shifting to look at how to gain preferential access by staying at the right hotels overseas, we look at the special case of Bethpage on Long Island.

Bethpage Black

The common belief is you have to camp out in the parking lot at Bethpage to secure a tee time on the Black Course. There are countless urban legends of how early you have to arrive, and the best methods of doing so. The procedures for getting a tee time have evolved over the years, and it has gotten easier for non–New York residents. If you do not want to wait in the parking lot, you register by faxing your driver's license and other personal details to the course, which is part of New York State's Park system. The details of how to do so are on the course's website. After you go through the process, you are assigned a registration number which you can use to book tee times through their automated telephone reservation system. The rules vary for New York residents and non-residents; residents have preference and can make reservations seven days in advance, which is a huge advantage. Non-residents can only make them two days in advance, which makes it hard to secure a time on the Black Course during the summer; therefore, the need to wait in line to play.

The first hour of tee times every day are reserved for "walk-ups," although it is more accurate to call them "sleep over" tee times. In addition to the first six groups every day, they allocate one foursome per hour for walk-ups. Your chances are better during the week than on the weekend; during the peak of the summer hopeful golfers start to wait in line midday the day before—and you do not technically stand in line, they have numbered parking spaces. The employees at the course hand out wristbands to those in line at an undisclosed time, and all the golfers who will be playing need to be present to receive their wristbands. It is not 100 percent predictable when they will hand them out, which is why you have to sleep in the parking lot; it can sometimes be the night before if they are expecting a lot of play; sometimes it is 6 a.m. the day of play; more typically it is between 4 a.m. and 5 a.m., so you have to be committed to do this.

The course is a stickler for following the rules, so even if you have a tee time, if you screw up they give your time away. Welcome to Long Island. You must arrive one hour before your tee time, so be prompt. This seems to be obvious enough, but if you have never driven on Long Island, you can't imagine how bad the traffic can sometimes be getting to and from the course, so better to be early than late.

Once you are through all the rigmarole of getting a tee time, your reward is one of the best courses in the world. It is one of Tillinghast's outstanding designs, is superbly maintained, and is a stern test of golf. Its formidable 15th hole is among the most challenging in the game; the hill you ascend to reach the green is so strikingly steep you can feel your hamstrings straining. The biggest downside is the pace of play—a five-and-a-half-hour round is not uncommon. One of my traveling golf partners is a

Bethpage Black's difficult 15th hole.

New York resident and he made a tee time without drama when I played. This is the best method if you know a New Yorker; if not, register on their system and play in the early spring or late fall during the week, when demand is lower. Take a caddie, because it is a hard course to walk, and because you'll have the full Long Island experience with a local; they have an endearing edginess bordering on abrasiveness. Folks from Long Island have a right to be proud, since mile-for-mile Long Island has a better collection of golf courses concentrated in a small area than anywhere in the world, and includes such courses as Shinnecock Hills, the National Golf Links, Maidstone, Sebonack, Friar's Head, Garden City Men's, Fishers Island, and Bethpage.

Europe

Shifting across the Atlantic, Valderrama, located in Southern Spain—very close to the Rock of Gibraltar—is a private club that has hosted the Ryder Cup won by Europe and captained by Seve Ballesteros. The club welcomes visitors as long as you play between noon and 2 p.m. The course is distinctive because it is routed through 2,000 cork trees, some of them directly in the line of play in the middle of fairways or blocking shots to the green. It is one of the only courses designed by Robert Trent Jones Sr. that I have played, and his design philosophy of "hard par, easy bogey" works well. Jaime Ortiz-Patiño, the mastermind behind Valderrama, was a billionaire and he invested great sums of money into the club, and it shows. It is one of the most meticulously maintained courses I have ever seen.

Also located in Spain is El Saler, which has fallen down in the world's rankings of late. There is a nice hotel and spa on site, Parador de El Saler. But the best reasons to visit are the topless bathers who sun themselves on the beach adjacent to the 8th hole, and the fact that it is situated in the handsome city of Valencia, and you can see the brilliant architecture of Santiago Calatrava, who was born and attended architecture school there.

The Turnberry Ailsa course on Scotland's West Coast is one of the more striking places you can play golf, with views as breathtaking as Pebble Beach's, and the easiest to reserve a tee time at of all the Open Championship courses. While it is possible

Valderrama's 2nd with approach shot through cork trees.

to play Turnberry without staying at the commanding hilltop resort overlooking the course, it is an integral part of the experience. Turnberry is one of the more recent courses to have been added to the Open rotation, having first hosted the tournament in only 1977, which was dramatically won by Tom Watson in the "Duel in the Sun" over Jack Nicklaus. I wholeheartedly agree with one of my favorite golf writers, Englishman Henry Longhurst, who wrote about Turnberry, "You find yourself lingering on the tee, gazing down on the waves as they break on the rocks and reflecting how good it is to be alive."

St. Andrews

Golfing at the Old Course at St. Andrews is a requisite part of every golfer's education because you have to play a unique style of golf there, different from almost anywhere else you play. The various entities, courses, and clubs in St. Andrews are confusing to understand so I will explain the differences up front. First, there is the R & A, one of the game's governing bodies, which is based in St. Andrews and runs the Open Championship. This is a separate entity than the St. Andrews Links Trust, which operates seven of the golf courses in St. Andrews including the Old Course, and it is a charitable organization. The Royal & Ancient Golf Club of St. Andrews is a separate entity still, also based in the town, and is a private club. The latter was founded in 1754 and has 2,400 members, the majority of whom are from Great Britain and Ireland. Their iconic clubhouse sits above the first hole on the Old Course and entry into the building is restricted to members and their guests.

St. Andrews is hallowed ground for golfers, although the course is disappointing on first sight. The ground is flat and featureless, the lies are tight and usually not good; it is not one of the most scenic courses, nor the most difficult. However, three of the greatest golfers of all time, Bobby Jones, Jack Nicklaus, and Tiger Woods, rank it at the top of their list of favorites. The Old Course reveals its alleged genius slowly, only after you play it again and again; the course has many hidden bunkers that you can't see while hitting your shots, particularly from the tees. The style of play is in contrast to what we have in the United States because there are no lush fairways, and firing at the pins would be the road to ruin at the Old Course.

Although golf has been played at St. Andrews for centuries, the course did not appear through a virgin birth. I like the comments of golf course architect Desmond Muirhead, who disputes the notion that the Old Course evolved without man's influence: "The truth is, the Old Course has been carefully manipulated with the same sort of refinement you might find in a Japanese garden."

Aside from the history, what makes the Old Course distinct from almost all other courses is best summed up again by Henry Longhurst, who writes, "What is the secret? Partly, I think that before playing any shot you have to stop and say to yourself, not, 'what club is it?' but 'what is it exactly that I am trying to do?' There are no fairways in the accepted sense of the word; just a narrow strip of golfing ground which you use both on the way out and the way in, together with huge double greens, each with two flags. From the tee you can play almost anywhere, but, if you have not thought it out correctly according to the wind and the position of the flag, you may find yourself teed up in the middle just behind a bunker, and downwind. At this point fools say the course is crazy. Others appreciate that the truth lies nearer home."

It is hard not to play the tourist at the Old Course and take a picture standing on the Swilcan Bridge and in front of the magnificent Royal & Ancient clubhouse. Regardless of who you are, hitting off the first tee on the Old Course is one of the most unforgettable and rewarding experiences a golfer can have in his or her lifetime; the fairway is probably the widest target in golf, but it is still a nerve-racking shot.

Despite all the golf history I have read and all the erudite people who admire the course, I still can't warm to it. It still appears flat and uninteresting to me, except the last four or five holes. It is fine to play it once to have the experience, but on subsequent visits I have found the course less interesting, not more. The tees are too close to the greens and you have to watch flying golf balls everywhere you turn, especially when near the holes around the Eden Estuary—Nos. 7 through 12—where several crisscross. Adding to the misery, rounds at the Old Course are normally agonizingly slow because of all the play it gets.

I know, I know, as Longhurst said, I'm a fool. And a heretic. "This guy doesn't get it, does he? How could he not like the Old Course?" Well, I live in New Jersey and I'm not a fan of Bruce Springsteen either, which is an offense punishable by death according to some. We all have differing tastes, and the Old Course and I do not mesh. I bring it up early in the book so if you'd like, you can throw it into your fireplace and be done with me straight away. I am not a St. Andrews hater; to the contrary, I appreciate a pair of courses there designed in the nineteenth-century: the New Course, a Tom Morris design built in 1895, and the Jubilee, built two years later. I appreciate the history and the university; I enjoy visiting the town and can see its alluring charms with eyes wide open. Given a choice, though, I would rather play nearby at Kingsbarns or at the best course in all of Europe—Carnoustie—if in the area, rather than at the Old Course.

A Tee Time at the Old Course

The most reliable way to reserve a tee time at the Old Course is through a tour operator—you book a minimum of three nights in a hotel and they reserve a time for you in advance. St. Andrews is dependent on golf for a good part of its livelihood, so the system is set up to ensure people stay in town and do not come and play the course for a day and leave. If you do not book through a tour you can apply for times in their daily lottery, or—if you are a long-range planner—once a year, for the following year in an annual lottery. You can also go early in the morning and stand in line for a single slot, which I have done, and it is amusing because you meet a wide variety of characters standing there for hours. Because the Old Course is common land, it is only open six days a week; it is closed on Sundays and used by all manner of people as a strolling— and dog walking—ground.

To summarize, there are four ways to book a tee time at the Old Course:

1. Book well in advance and pay one of the tour operators for access. This requires that you stay in the town of St. Andrews for three nights. The effective cost of your round is hard to calculate because the packages begin at $3,500, or over $1,000 per night. This option is called "The Old Course Experience," and you play two other courses in town, which is included in your steep fee.

2. Walk up and stand in line early as a single and your chances of getting out depend on the season. I tried this one cold October morning and arrived at 6 a.m. I was the fifteenth person in line and played at around 1:30 p.m., so I counsel patience. The frost-bitten vicar who was first in line arrived at 2:30 a.m. and had a sleeping bag. He played around 10 a.m.

3. You can apply to the daily lottery—ballot as they call it—where one-half the tee times are allotted forty-eight-hours in advance. The cost to play the Old Course this way is about $250. George Peper, in his entertaining book about St. Andrews, estimates the chances of winning the lottery to be about 35 percent in season and 95 percent off-season, the latter basically being the winter—November through March— when you have to play on plastic mats that protect the turf. My guess is these odds are about right having tried the lottery a couple of times in season without success. Results

for the lottery are posted online every day at 4 p.m. and they show tee times and the names of players going out. The St. Andrews website is a good place to visit if you are ever bored and need to kill some time, you can check and see if you know anybody going out to play.

4. If you can plan a year ahead, they have an advanced reservations process—which runs from August 27 through September 15 of each year—and you submit your name in a ballot to play the following year. It is unclear how many times they reserve for this method.

Their byzantine rules are all outlined on their complex website in cryptic detail. All the tee times for the Old Course are not allocated to the general public because there are many local golf clubs in town that have access to the course. Some tee times are also allocated to hotels in town (the Burness House and the Russell Hotel), although gaining access to them is typically quite expensive. A handicap below twenty-four is needed for men to play, and below thirty-six for women.

Muirfield

Another of the elite clubs in the world sits across the bay from St. Andrews on the—phonetically pleasantly named—Firth of Forth: Muirfield. As I mentioned in the opening chapter, it is one of those places that ticks all the boxes, and is the third-highest ranked course in the world. It holds such a venerated place in the world of golf because the Honourable Company drew up the original thirteen rules of golf. The course was originally designed by Old Tom Morris, with major revisions made by H. S. Colt and minor ones made by Tom Simpson. A list of past Open Champions at Muirfield reads like a roster of the game's Hall of Fame and includes Harry Vardon, James Braid, Walter Hagen, Tom Watson, Jack Nicklaus, Gary Player, Sir Nick Faldo, Ernie Els, and Phil Mickelson. More than an average golf club, in many ways they are still one of the driving forces keeping up the traditions of the game.

Muirfield allows guest play but restricts it to three foursomes on Tuesdays and Thursdays and limits men to a maximum handicap of eighteen. As a result, securing a tee time at Muirfield requires you to plan well in advance since demand exceeds supply. When you book a round I recommend staying for the day to soak up the whole experience, which includes playing your own ball in the morning, having lunch in the member's dining room, and playing alternate shot in the afternoon; it is one of the most memorable days of golf you can experience. Guests are permitted to tee off between 8:30 a.m. and 10 a.m., and only from the 10th tee. For the morning round you are allowed to play your own ball, but they only take bookings for four people, since no singles, twosomes, or threesomes are permitted. Inside the clubhouse a jacket and tie are required in the dining room and smoking room and cameras are not permitted. Make sure you are deferential to the club "secretary," as managers are known here.

When I played, after completing the morning round we changed back into jacket and tie and made our way to the member's dining room for a proper lunch. Although the Scots are better known for their full breakfast, lunch at the Honourable Company is an experience in indulgence. The dining room is oblong in shape and contains a series of long slender tables where you eat cafeteria-style, although this doesn't capture the appropriate sense of decorum. It's along the lines of a prep-school dining hall, only with a touch more class. The walls are lined with pictures of past captains of the Honourable Company and at the end of the room are oversized glass windows overlooking the course.

The cornucopia of food is organized into multiple sections, each representing a separate course: drinks and spirits, soup, carvery, cheeses, and sweets. You sit at the galley tables next to strangers, including members, and gorge yourself. The room is steamy because of the water baths and heat lamps, but you wouldn't dare take off your jacket or loosen your tie for fear of being scolded: stiff-upper-lip, never let them see you sweat, as the saying goes—surely, the originator of the expression must have been a member who sat here suffering with prickly heat? It is the custom at the Honourable Company that the captain of the club wears a red jacket, comparable to Augusta's green jackets, although at Muirfield the tradition is much older. After our lunch, we took the indulgence they encourage to the extreme, waddled into the smoking room, sat in sumptuous leather chairs overlooking the 18th green, and had cocktails.

After cocktails, we played foursomes (alternate shot), which is the mandatory afternoon format for visitors and the overall preferred format at Muirfield. One of the delights of alternate shot is that you can play in two and a half hours. While initially our group was moaning because we wanted to play our own balls, in the end, we wouldn't have had the same experience without it. The format is highly recommend and there is much to be learned from a club that has been playing golf for over two hundred and fifty years.

A little-known way to secure a tee time a Muirfield—beyond the sparing two dozen per week they allocate to the public—is to stay at the Greywalls Hotel. The Greywalls is symbiotic with Muirfield. Originally a manor home, it was built as a holiday retreat for a member of the Weaver family who was a keen golfer, and was converted into a

Greywalls Hotel, Muirfield, Scotland with the golf course behind it *(Inverlochy Castle Management, Scotland)*.

hotel in 1928. Designed by the well-known Edwardian architect Sir Edwin Lutyens, it is a beauty and enjoys protected preservation status as a historic building. The hotel is made even more enticing because its extraordinary gardens were designed by the influential British garden designer Gertrude Jekyll. The Greywalls and Muirfield are hard to tell apart, and there is even a doorway connecting the Greywalls to Muirfield. On Monday and Friday mornings an undisclosed number of tee times are given to select guests who stay a minimum of two nights. My experience at the all-male Muirfield was a lesson in golf tradition. We played the 10th hole during our morning round (our first hole) and were about to tee off on the 11th when our caddies became flustered. Since we were the second group out that day we had seasoned caddies, one of whom noticed the group behind us was four women, who are not allowed to play together without a gentleman. "If the secretary sees this he will throw both groups off the course and fire the caddies." Their husbands were behind them on the 10th tee planning to play as a group. True to tradition, our most senior caddie approached the group on the 10th green and made them split up. At Muirfield, a rule is a rule.

CHAPTER FIVE

The Courses of the British Isles, Australia, New Zealand, and Canada

More than half of the most elite private clubs and courses in the world will let you play without knowing a member, and your usual foursome can come along to play. The most important document you need is your passport. Not surprisingly, since it was the birthplace of the game, there are scores of sought-after and desirable places to play golf in the British Isles. Two dozen of the courses I played on my journey were there, and they are some of the most memorable and interesting ones. Courses located throughout the Commonwealth countries also welcome visitor play including those in South Africa, New Zealand, and Australia.

As I noted earlier, private golf clubs in the United States generally operate as tax-exempt entities, and those receiving more than 35 percent of total revenues from outside their membership would either subject themselves to taxation or lose their tax-exempt status. The structure of clubs outside the United States differs, and while many are still tax-exempt entities, they do not have the same limitations as clubs in the United States. Part of the way they circumvent it is when playing their courses, you become a temporary member; that is, a member for the day. Thus, they have not generated revenue from non-member activities. Aside from the tax reasons, I also think United States golf evolved with less open traditions.

Ganton Golf Club

While there are a couple of exceptions to the rule that I cover in a future chapter, the basic method to playing outside the United States is to request a date and time to play. I will illustrate the case by doing a deep-dive into Ganton Golf Club, which is located in the lush Yorkshire countryside in Northeast England, with its rolling hills and unspoiled moors. A private club founded in 1891, Ganton has a rich history. It is the course where Harry Vardon served as the professional between 1896 and 1903. Vardon was one of the greatest players of all time, having won the Open Championship six times and the US Open once, at the historic Chicago Golf Club. Ted Ray, winner of the Open Championship at Muirfield and the US Open at Inverness in Ohio, also served as the head professional at Ganton. Some of golf's most esteemed architects have had a hand in shaping the course, including J. H. Taylor, H. S. Colt, Alister MacKenzie, and James Braid. The Ganton railway station, now gone, was 300 yards from the course, and when it was operating, caddies used to meet their players at the station and accompany them to the clubhouse. The course has also hosted three British Amateur championships, the 2003 Walker Cup, and the 1949 Ryder Cup, won by the United States and captained by Ben Hogan. The course's distinguishing features are its setting in idyllic surroundings, its strategic nature, its irrationally deep bunkers, and an impossible 251-yard par-3 17th hole. Although it is unknown to many people in the United States, it can't be denied that Ganton holds a storied place in the world of golf.

Ganton, England, with its signature deep bunkering.

The simple way to play Ganton is to go to their website and look at their booking procedure. The most important aspect of booking outside the United States is to show the proper respect and to follow the club's rules. In Ganton's case they make tee times available during the week and on weekends, and their greens fees are £95 (approximately $150) during the week and slightly more on the weekend. It is such a refreshing approach to visitors; can you imagine going to Riviera's website and booking a tee time to play on Saturday afternoon?

Playing overseas is different than at home and there are many quirks, particularly when you play in England. Of particular note are the quirky rules many clubs provide about attire. Ganton provides advice on how to dress and they advise gentlemen they may wear tailored shorts with knee-length "single colour" socks. Denim jeans, collarless shirts, and training shoes are not permitted on the course or in the clubhouse, although, if they have to tell you, you shouldn't be trying to play. You are permitted to wear your golf attire—assuming you change back into your street shoes—inside the clubhouse, except in the Vardon room or in the member's dining room, in which case you need to wear a jacket and tie after 10:30 a.m. Their dress code lays out their wonderfully eccentric exception: "It is accepted that some young gentlemen under sixteen years of age may not have jackets. In such cases, when in the company of a parent, grandparent, or a member *in loco parentis*, a shirt and tie with or without a long sleeved pullover is acceptable." Ganton upholds the standards and traditions of proper English clubs and is old-school, which is to be treasured; their locker room has old-fashioned style separate hot and cold water faucets, the television is tuned to the BBC, and the course is surrounded by beautiful English hedges that grow so vigorously here.

You can rent a pull cart or "hand trolley," as they call them, but I advise taking caddies wherever you can because they add so much color to your round and can help guide you on where to hit the ball and assist in reading greens. Except at resorts, golf carts are almost non-existent in the British Isles, which is a good tradition from my viewpoint. Golf is a walking game, and similar to Oakmont's policy, Ganton will let you take a "buggy" only if you have a note from a doctor. Ganton has no sprinkler heads with yardage markers on them; you can buy a yardage book if you want, but basically you have to look, judge the wind, and hit the ball.

Somewhat unusual for the British Isles, Ganton has a driving range; many of the courses I have played in Ireland, England, and Scotland do not, which is one of the charms of playing here and makes for some interesting first holes. For the record, the folks at Ganton are some of the nicest and most accommodating in the world of golf; on both my visits I was treated well and felt they were truly happy to have me visiting.

I recommend having lunch or post-round snacks while visiting. You can usually order a nice selection of finger, or tea sandwiches, normally with the ends of the bread cut off. Standards are ham, egg mayonnaise (egg salad) on brown bread, cucumber, chicken and watercress, or roast beef with classic English mustard. Or, if you are so inclined, you can have sausages and cakes with tea after the round, as a hearty group sitting nearby us did the last time I visited. "Toasties" are on the menu throughout the Isles, basically a grilled ham or cheese sandwich, as are "bacon baps," and my own personal favorite, the "Haggis & Cheese" special at Royal Dornoch. My preference while visiting the British Isles is to have a proper Guinness after the round. There are many myths about why it tastes better there than at home, including the fact that it is not pasteurized (it is); it is simply fresher closer to the source, and because they are such a beer-centric society they take the time to clean the pipes properly.

The other delightful aspect about playing golf in the British Isles is the hotels. With a couple of exceptions—such as staying in London, Belfast, or Dublin—the hotels tend to be more local, quirky, and personalized than those in the United States. Chains are not dominant here and the best places to stay are bed-and-breakfasts, which I have had success finding on TripAdvisor.com. "Country House" hotels are delightful when far from the big cities, as are "Marine" hotels, which are found more commonly by the seaside, where many of the courses are located. They make up in charm what they lack beyond basic accommodation.

Sunningdale

Ganton is one of the easier courses to book into because they have a liberal visitor policy. Let's now shift and look at some other clubs. Sunningdale Golf Club, located on the outskirts of London, is another of my favorites. As their website describes them,

"Sunningdale is the quintessential English Club and as close to Augusta National as any club in the British Isles. Golf is the only thing that matters at Sunningdale." The Old Course at Sunningdale was designed by Willie Park Jr. in 1901 and was tinkered with over the years by H. S. Colt, who served as the secretary. A 36-hole club, Colt co-designed the equally superb New Course, built in 1923. Sunningdale is a heathland course set on sandy soil and dotted with birch trees, pines, heather, and gorse. Golf is sometimes referred to metaphorically as a walk in the park; in the case of Sunningdale, it is literally true. The course is surrounded by deep woods and is idyllic and peaceful. It has a stately English clubhouse, a "Stockbroker's Tudor," and there are walking paths around the course where people stroll with their dogs in peaceful solitude. Sunningdale

Sunningdale, Ascot, England, 6th hole, Old Course.

has some deep Bobby Jones history; it was on Sunningdale's Old Course during an Open Championship qualifier in 1926 that Jones shot what was described as a "perfect" round. The standard scratch score on the course at the time was 75. He shot a 66, with a 33 on the front and a 33 on the back; he had 33 full shots and 33 putts; the highest number written on his scorecard was a four. This feat is even more incredible if put into its proper context. He was using hickory-shafted clubs and a golf ball that was nowhere near those of today's standards. The course wasn't exactly short either; on ten holes he hit his shot to the green with a two-iron or a wood.

To book tee times at Sunningdale you contact the secretary, and their greens fees are about double Ganton's during peak season, or £205 (approximately $300). Sun-

Sunningdale's Stockbroker's Tudor clubhouse and the 18th green, Old Course.

ningdale restricts guest play to Monday through Thursday; you have to pay in advance, and if you cancel within three months of your tee time you lose the entire fee. On the positive side, toasted tea cakes and crumpets are served from 2:30 p.m. to 6 p.m. in the bar. Sunningdale's sock rule is "plain coloured knee length socks or white sports socks which cover the ankle." Similar to a fair number of elite private clubs around the world, Sunningdale has a security gate at the entrance and you are advised to check with the secretary a week before you play to obtain the current security code.

Visiting Sunningdale is one of the finer experiences in the world of private club golf. There are few things more satisfying than sitting in the Stockbroker's Tudor after a round with a pint in hand, reflecting back on a brilliant day's golf. Sunningdale is among a small group of clubs that combine the best of everything: a world-class set of golf courses with a historic, warm, and inviting club. Bobby Jones sums up the course succinctly, and it captures my sentiments ideally, "It's a wonderful course, Sunningdale, I wish I could carry it about with me. I wanted to bring it back home."

My first two examples of booking in the United Kingdom were at clubs that are intimate and inviting. As I said, some are more inviting than others, and the Wentworth Club, outside of London, is less so, and a bit more difficult. As headquarters of the PGA Tour Europe it is a large club, has tennis and other activities, and feels more corporate than most clubs you can visit here. Nevertheless, its West Course, designed by H. S. Colt, is world-renowned and worth a visit, although their visitors' greens fees between May 1 and October are an outrageously steep £360 (approximately $550).

The Joy of Travel

I have traveled to the British Isles many times and they are some of the best trips a group of golfers can take. Not only do you visit world-class courses, but playing day after day puts you into a rhythm that is hypnotic: have breakfast, play a round of golf at an exclusive club or two, followed by your après-round drinks and a nice dinner; top it off with a stay in an idiosyncratic B & B, and you have a winning formula. After a couple of days you start to truly relax and lose track of what day of the week it is; you begin to imagine dropping out of society and doing this week after week, and never tiring of it. As compared to a trip to a United States resort, it is orders of magnitude better.

One of the first decisions on a trip overseas is whether to drive or not. The answer depends on whether you are comfortable driving a manual transmission car in the rain, on the wrong side of the road, on no sleep after taking a red-eye flight the night before. Personally I relish it, and it is one of the enjoyable aspects of visiting here. Many people hire a driver, particularly if they have a larger group, and that can add a lot of spice to your trip. On one of my many trips to Ireland we had a group of eight crammed into a van built for six, without padded seats. Our driver was a farmer whose crops had failed; he had a poor sense of direction and intense body odor, although he was such an endearing man that we all came to adore him. On another trip we had a driver who was a drummer in a jazz band who had a self-made CD on continuous loop for a week—of what we believed was the same song—playing over and over and over. I can still hear the repetitive tune in my head to this day. The other question is whether to book all the travel, hotels, drivers, and golf yourself or whether to use a tour. As a control freak, I prefer to do it myself and enjoy interacting with the clubs beforehand, but there are experienced golf tour operators that can setup the trip, arrange your transport, and secure you tee times.

Britain

As you have no doubt noticed, I love the eccentricity of the British and am a certified Anglophile. George Bernard Shaw hit the nail on the head when he said, "England and America are two countries divided by a common language." Across the Atlantic, after dinner, you do not have dessert, they bring a sweets trolley; you're not having a bad day, you're "off the boil." The roundabout (traffic circle) is one of the greatest road inventions in the world. Out in the countryside in remote villages, I receive great joy driving by a red phone box standing on the side of the road in isolation; I love the BBC, the pomp and circumstance of the Royals, and all the rules and respect for authority. Plus, you have to admire a people who know how to properly stand in line without cutting in; their "queue" system is a thing of wonder. I have an affinity for their television shows, particularly the old Morse detective show, the *Rumpole of the Bailey* series, and *Downton Abbey*. I adore Monty Python, the Beatles, Colman's mustard, English gardens, and the smell of a peat fire burning in the distance when playing golf, as well as Wimbledon and the Open Championship.

For a country with so much reputed hierarchy and class distinction, I find it rather open and inviting; after all, you can play all their top championship venues and they let you visit their best private clubs. I am drawn to their simplicity; unlike many clubs in the United States, they are much understated. Locker rooms are not lined with four types of painkiller, there is no talc, and there are not row-upon-row of aftershave or razors; just the basics.

As for the golf, they understand the critical true nature of the game, which is that it should be played fast. And match play should be the predominant form of the game because it is more fun and you play faster by not having to putt everything out. Most golf here is match play and handicaps are established on the basis of your "medal play" rounds, which occur only occasionally. Also, the game played here is primarily on the ground with bump and run shots being a key part of a golfer's repertoire. Their courses are not overly manicured and you'll have more than an occasional bad bounce—rub on the green, as they say. I can count on one hand the number of times I have hit a lob wedge while playing in Britain because the lies are so tight.

I am also a big fan of their full breakfast; these people know how to eat in the morning with their standard fare of eggs, bacon, sausage, blood pudding, tomatoes, baked beans, potatoes, and toast. Every trip I have ever made here I have savored a "full-fry" and raised my cholesterol level by ten points. Having dinner at a country house hotel surely has to be one of the most civilized of all dining experiences. While sitting in the drawing room having cocktails your server gives you menus; you order your meal, and when the first course is ready you are summoned to the dining room. "Common land" is a concept that doesn't exist at home and it allows people to walk through some otherwise private and exclusive golf courses. I remember playing at the Royal North Devon Golf Club, the oldest in England; the course is named Westward Ho! and it is one of the distinct experiences in golf because it is built on common land. There were horses walking across the first couple of holes, sheep grazing on fairways

Woodhall Spa, England, 15th hole *(Graylyn Loomis)*.

along the back nine, and people walking dogs throughout the course—who have the right of way. Similarly, it adds tremendously to the charm of a place to see families out for a Sunday stroll walking across the course, which I also experienced at both Woodhall Spa near Sherwood Forest in Northern England, and at St. Enodoc in Cornwall in Southwest England.

After our round of golf at Ganton the last time I was there, we stopped at a local pub so we could make the day last longer and continue to savor the experience. The locals welcomed us warmly as night fell and it became chilly outside; the bartender lit a coal-burning fire, which I had never sat in front of before, and it was delightful, although it can singe your eyebrows from a good five feet away. The pub culture is still alive and well in England, and as we usually are, we were embraced, entertained to no end, and regaled with story after story.

Another option available when playing at Britain's storied courses is staying at a Dormy House. I did this when I visited Royal Lytham & St. Annes, eleven-time host to the Open Championship. At Lytham they restrict visitor play to Mondays and Thursdays, although they will let you play late in the day on other days. A Dormy House is a separate building on the property that has bedrooms; Ritz Carlton–style rooms these are not, Dormy being a derivative of the word dormitory, although they are basic and clean, and you share showers. It is a recommended experience where you can do it because it saves you from driving after the round; you can hang back in the clubhouse, enjoy a pint of Guinness and dinner, and then go to the Dormy house, play pool, and reminisce about the day's golf.

Cruden Bay

In my experience, it is the unexpected discoveries that end up making traveling for golf such an intriguing endeavor. Unexpected and unique, such as the *sui generis* Cruden Bay Golf Club, located along the Aberdeen coast in Scotland. When I first walked to the end of the parking lot and looked down on the course I was startled; it was unlike any golf course I had ever seen. The course defies being pigeonholed; it is one-of-a-kind. Golf at its simplest is a game, and I think we sometimes lose sight of that fact. The world of golf has much sterner tests than Cruden Bay, but for pure fun it cannot be beaten. The course would be ranked number one in the world if having fun was the only criterion utilized. When I first played Cruden Bay early in my golf travels, I experienced what the French call *coup de foudre*, which translates into "a thunderbolt," or more accurately, love at first sight. There is something about Cruden Bay that brightens your mood. It made me see golf through the eyes of a five-year-old—everything is exciting, there is a sense of discovery around every corner, life is good and full of promise, curiosity abounds.

Cruden Bay was originally designed by Old Tom Morris and then redesigned by Tom Simpson and Herbert Fowler in 1926. The course is routed through massive sand

Cruden Bay, Scotland, the 14th hole with a "bathtub" green.

dunes and can generously be described as unorthodox. Its 14th hole has a sunken, hidden "bathtub" green that has to be seen to be believed, followed by a 231-yard blind par-3 that plays over an enormous sand dune. You have to ring a bell when you are done playing because the group behind can't see you. Bernard Darwin, the dean of English golf writers, wrote of this charming course, "I think it is typical of Cruden Bay, which is a place extraordinarily difficult to keep away from for those who have once come under its spell." I was often asked what I was going to do when I was done playing the top 100 courses and one of my responses was I was going to go back to Cruden Bay to play it over and over again. I have yet to do so but at some point I will block out a week and go over and soak up every minute of it. Although a private club, Cruden Bay is easy to access. You can visit their website for booking details.

British and Irish Caddies

I wanted to highlight Cruden Bay both because it is such a tantalizing course, but also because it has a tradition I have never seen in the United States. Due to its remote nature, its members serve as caddies. The arrangement works well because their fee is modest, you can learn about the course, and obviously they know the greens. One of my caddies at Cruden Bay would not allow a ball to be lost; he would dive deep into gorse bushes in search of wayward balls despite our pleas that he didn't have to. It was a point of pride for him, and he found every one. I believe British people to be much more polite generally than Americans. Whereas a caddie at Bethpage might tell you that you hit a bad shot, over here they are more deferential. A ball that you slice wildly out of bounds might receive an "Oooooh . . . that's touch and go." In their efforts to be respectful, silence is the most telling response of all. You know your ball is definitively lost when they say nothing at all, although sometimes they can't help themselves. After failing to take instruction, I hit one downhill putt so hard at Cruden Bay that my caddie started running after the ball shouting, "No, John, no . . . no . . . no."

Another Scottish course where the members are caddies is the Crail Golfing Society outside of St. Andrews, the seventh-oldest golf club in the world. I had one of my best caddies ever there, a giant of a man named Jack. Doing mental arithmetic in his head wasn't one of his fortes; he carried around a little notebook and pencil and calculated the yardage distances by hand every time I would ask. I would walk up to a ball five yards behind a 150-yard marker and say, "What do you think, Jack?" He would take out his paper, calculate the number, and tell me on a thirty-second delay it was 145! He was a kindhearted man and joined us in the clubhouse afterward telling story after story while drinking half pints of beer, after each one saying, "This is my last one, I have to go see my mum." He also was not a big fan of the Old Course at St. Andrews and told us about a dozen times, maybe more, "The Old Course is shite, and a lot of locals are afraid to tell you for fear of getting in trouble." To this day, the first thought that pops into my mind when someone brings up the Old Course is Jack's description of it.

Caddies are not always deferential. My caddie at Carnoustie had a wickedly dry Scottish sense of humor. As soon as I hit my ball on the par-3 8th hole he laughed heartily in my face, turned to the other caddies, and said, "That's O. B. Wan Kenobi," using a *Star Wars* line. Despite his antics, he was one of the best caddies I ever had. He was a master at reading greens and received a lovely tip. I played Gullane's No. 1 course in Scotland one uncharacteristically hot day when it was crowded. The wind was not blowing at all, which is bad over here because the midges—tiny, almost invisible flies—were eating us alive. We had to wait on the group ahead of us to hit every shot. To make matters worse, my dear friend and playing partner, Sheldon, was hit by a ball in the knee during the round. A caddie from the group behind approached us at about the 14th hole and said, "The secretary of the club requests you play faster," to which Sheldon-with-the-swollen-knee responded, "You can tell the secretary of the club to go 'F' himself," although he used all four letters, reinforcing every stereotype of bad-mannered American golfers. The caddie was trying to work two loops that day, which you can't blame him for, although we clearly weren't the problem.

My greatest caddie of all was at Royal Portrush in Northern Ireland, a fidgety chain-smoker of hand-rolled cigarettes. Putts I hit firmly were met with a gasp of "steamy," and on the 9th hole I asked him what the yardage was. He said it was 150 yards; I was in between clubs and asked what he thought about me playing it 160 yards. His simple reply was "There's no flag at 160," as he handed me my 150-yard club, turned his back and walked away. A caddie saved my round when I played Royal Dornoch in the Scottish Highlands for the first time. Dornoch is an out-and-back layout and I had a case of the shanks as we were playing the holes farthest from the clubhouse. As Henry Longhurst has said about the dreaded shot, "It is the most demeaning shot in golf, perhaps in any sport." In any event, I wasn't feeling particularly good about myself and wanted to quit. I asked if there was a pro I could see to have him look at my swing. His reply was typical of the Scots, succinct and to the point: "You don't need a pro, turn your shoulder and hit the fookin ball," and he was right. He guided in a fragile golfer for the rest of the round, and I am eternally grateful.

The Royals

Dornoch is one of the world's finest clubs and is worth focusing on because it highlights another tradition in United Kingdom golf. The course was designed in 1886 by Old Tom Morris and although it was subsequently changed by others, it had a great beginning. Donald Ross was born in Dornoch and served as its professional and its greenkeeper at one time. There are few places—Royal County Down comes to mind also—as beautiful to play when the yellow gorse is in bloom, and, although hard to travel to, it is a treat. The club's rules are accommodating and their own particular list of no-nos include wearing, "Wet clothing, T-Shirts, or Rugby tops," in the clubhouse. One of their well thought-out rules is that only two-ball matches can play before 9 a.m. At first, we were a bit irritated by the rule because we didn't want to break our routine. Similar to Muirfield's alternate-shot rule, it is based on tradition and it promotes a brisk pace of play; you are finished playing golf well before lunch and ready to go out and soak up the course again.

Even more stringent than Dornoch, the Rye Golf Club in Southeast England won't allow you to play in a typical American-style fourball match, and, unusual for the United Kingdom, you need to find a member to play. As their club's policy succinctly outlines, "All play is in two-ball format with foursomes preferred in the morning. No three or fourball golf is played. No tee time system is operated. Invitations to visiting golfers are made at the secretary's discretion."

I have had almost universally good experiences when traveling through the British Isles. One exception was at Royal Troon, which has one of the more prickly set of rules. They allow visitors on Mondays, Tuesdays, and Thursdays. When I visited, they shoved us into a small, crowded dining room with bland cafeteria-grade food; almost all the other clubs I have been to treat you as a member for a day, let you order off the menu, and make you feel welcome. Troon was the unfortunate exception.

I am dwelling on the dress restrictions because the clubs take them seriously, especially those with a "Royal" designation. Royal Aberdeen in Scotland is an old and traditional club that was formed before the US Constitution was signed. Their rules state, in all capital letters no less, "shorts or cargo style trousers, jeans, trainers and tee shirts are UNACCEPTABLE on the course and in the clubhouse." We played there on a day when the temperature was about seventy-two degrees, which is warm for Scotland. Sheldon wasn't paying attention before we left for the course and wore shorts; the rest of our group wore long pants. They wouldn't let him play and consulted with the secretary. As a compromise, and because he is such a good-looking gentleman, they let him buy a huge pair of socks in the pro shop that came up above his knees, and he joined us. They invoked the little-known "long sock" rule of their bylaws, as we now jokingly call it.

I would be remiss if I didn't mention two old-world Scottish clubs: North Berwick and Prestwick. When many of the budding golf course architects of the twentieth century traveled across the Atlantic to study, they visited these two gems, as do many of today's aspiring architects. Old Tom Morris served as the

Prestwick, Scotland, 1st hole ("Railway").

Keeper of the Green at Prestwick, and the club has hosted the Open Championship a total of twenty-four times. Some of the most timeless designs for holes are here, including an Alps hole and a Cardinal hole. It has the best opening hole in golf, in my view, with a stone wall and railway line running the length of the hole down the right side. North Berwick, located on the East Coast of Scotland, features the original and oft-copied Redan hole, and has several holes you play over and around stone walls. Both are hospitable to visitors and my adulation for them is exceptionally high. Be sure to stay for the fantastic lunch Prestwick serves in the member dining room.

Courses throughout Ireland and Northern Ireland follow the same basic process as those in Scotland and England and are most accommodating. While about 95 percent of clubs in the United Kingdom allow visitors, there are some that have much more restrictive policies for visitors, more akin to American clubs. The anachronistic Swinley Forest has no website, and similar to Rye, to play, you need to find a member. Membership is passed down from generation to generation and many are members of the landed gentry. HRH the Duke of York is a member of Swinley Forest and a portion of the land the course occupies is leased from the Crown Estate (the Royal Family). Their club history boasts that it is easier to have a papal audience than it is to be invited to play, although they do allow visiting Golfing Societies. The US Ambassador to Great Britain is given a membership to Swinley when serving, so you could always use your diplomatic connections to try to play.

Canada

This hockey-obsessed country follows the same basic methodology as the United States, with most private courses requiring you to find a member as your host. World-ranked courses in Toronto include the magnificent Stanley Thompson–designed St. George's Golf & Country Club and the H. S. Colt–designed Hamilton Golf & Country Club. Around Montreal, Mount Bruno is known for its below-the-radar charm and has a golf course that was designed by one of my favorite designers, Willie Park Jr.—who also designed Maidstone and Sunningdale's Old Course.

New Zealand

Golf in the Southern Hemisphere follows the same basic model as in the British Isles, which is good, because it has some of the best clubs and courses in the world. New Zealand is a logical place to start because two of the clubs are resort-style and easy to book. The brainchild of billionaire Julian Robertson, both Kauri Cliffs and Cape Kidnappers quickly make you forget the long journey. Both offer on-site lodges, with Kidnappers having the more rustic accommodations and Kauri having as high-end a facility as can be imagined. Kauri's lodge, about $850 a night, was a bit rich for me, so while there I stayed at local bed-and-breakfasts which were fantastic. Both courses are built up on high headlands with vertigo-inducing cliffs as high as 500 feet that plunge down to the Pacific Ocean, and are sumptuous places to play golf. I am most grateful for having been able to make the long journey to play them.

Paraparaumu Beach Golf Club is located near Wellington—the Southern Hemisphere's San Francisco, with steep hills and incomparable views—and although a private club, follows the United Kingdom model and allows visitors to book easily. All three courses noted thus far are on the North Island. I enthusiastically recommend visiting the South Island also, specifically Queenstown, which is one of the most breathtaking cities in the world. Jack's Point, located there, is essential to visit, and as a public course, it is easy to book. The course was designed in 2008 by Kiwi John Darby, who studied golf and landscape architecture at Harvard. After seeing what he designed here, I would say he graduated with honors. Darby's design philosophy is a simple one: "look hard, play easy."

Jack's Point has one of my favorite holes, the unconventional 15th. The walk from the 14th green to the 15th tee at Jack's Point is up a small incline, and when you reach the crest of the hill there is a hand-fitted rough-hewn stone wall, the first on the course. A peek over the top of the wall reveals a 383-yard uphill dogleg right par-4 gem. The tee box is built above a high meadow and the golfer must hit a forced carry over it, to a long fairway set at an angle to the tee box. I remember back to my initial visit to North Berwick when I was awestruck over the placement of the stone walls. The stone wall here frames an elevated fairway and is part of a sheep paddock. If your drive doesn't carry the stone wall and ends up in the paddock, you may be able to find your

Jack's Point, Queenstown, New Zealand, 15th hole.

ball because the area is still grazed. The 15th is a classic risk-reward hole that dares the golfer to take an aggressive line left, with a severe penalty for missing. The approach shot to the well-bunkered green plays a couple of clubs longer because the green sits about thirty feet above the fairway. Do not be surprised to find yourself hitting two balls off the tee even if your first drive is in a good position; the hole is that much fun. When I mentioned this to Darby, he said he does the same when playing the course.

It is easy to overuse superlatives when describing top golf courses, but New Zealand's South Island has such stunning unspoiled beauty even without any golf. The air is unimaginably pure, the water seems bluer than other water, and the natural lakes in the region look like they were airbrushed in. Jack's Point takes advantage of its location in the midst of a mountain range—appropriately called "The Remarkables"—to a degree that is almost inconceivable, and I will take the pleasant memories of visiting with me to the grave.

Australia

Australia has some of the best private club golfs in the world, beginning with the Alister MacKenzie designed Royal Melbourne. There are two courses at Royal Melbourne, the West and the East, both world-class. A composite course, made up of a majority of holes from the West and a few from the East, is ranked among the twenty-five best courses in the world, although visitors aren't normally allowed to play the composite; it is used only for championships or occasionally there are designated days for amateur tournaments when they allow play. For a club held in such high esteem around the world, Royal Melbourne warmly welcomes visitors, but they have a bit of a twist from the courses in the British Isles. At Royal Melbourne you need a "letter of introduction" from your home club; basically, something your pro can give you noting that you are a member in good standing and stating your handicap. You receive your "honorary member" bag tag when visiting and are granted full privileges, including the ability to eat in the clubhouse. The normal greens fee rate is A$300 (approximately $290).

I played both courses at Royal Melbourne on the same day for free. At the time, the course was undergoing renovations in preparation for the 2011 Presidents Cup matches and therefore was not in the usual condition they expect, so they didn't feel it was right to charge us. To be honest, the course was in tip-top shape. They must have extremely high standards if the conditions we played in weren't considered good. This was a classy move on the part of Royal Melbourne; thank you again for your generosity.

The Kingston Heath Golf Club, located near Royal Melbourne, has a similar policy, and requires a letter of introduction, as does the New South Wales Golf Club, near Sydney. The latter has some holes on the Pacific Ocean with forced carries over headlands that are reminiscent of Cypress Point. The other private course I played in

Royal Adelaide Golf Club, South Australia, 7th hole.

Australia and enjoyed immensely is Royal Adelaide—which Alister MacKenzie had a hand in designing—located in the state of South Australia. It has several peculiarities. Because Adelaide is in the interior of the country, they set their clock to the half-hour. When it is 3 p.m. in Sydney and Melbourne, it is only 2:30 p.m. in Adelaide. The course has an active train running through it, which, far from being annoying, I found to be charming, and the course's iron-rich soil has a reddish hue, giving the land a rusty look. Adelaide is an inviting city, with a concentration of Victorian-era buildings and a Napa-esque wine growing region nearby.

Royal Adelaide has a train running through the middle of the course.

There is golf on Australia's mainland and then there is Tasmania, a world apart. A remote island and an exotic land off Australia's south coast, it is worth trekking to. Aside from being an interesting cultural experience, it has some spectacular golf, specifically the Tom Doak designed Barnbougle Dunes and the Coore & Crenshaw designed Lost Farms, both of which are resort courses and easy to book into. You can stay right on property in their rustic lodges at a fraction of the price of staying at Kauri Cliffs or Cape Kidnappers. The 4th hole at Barnbougle is without question one of the finest golf holes ever built. A short par-4, it plays only 270 yards, but into the prevailing wind. If the wind is not blowing or is blowing downwind, it would be a drivable green.

A massive bunker on the right side of the fairway gets the mind going with negative possibilities; I imagine plenty of shots are pulled left as the golfer panics at the last second thinking about the oversized hazard, which is a naturally-blown bunker. If you hit short of the large bunker you have a steep uphill shot to a green you can't fully see. The second shot plays to an extremely well-protected and crazy green. Although his inspiration for this hole was Royal Melbourne West's 10th, when Doak designed it he must have been on some kind of mind-altering drug; it is a sick hole and joyous to play.

After completing the 4th at Barnbougle, the walk to the 5th tee is a fair distance, up a big sand dune, and when you reach the crest of the hill Bass Strait comes into

Barnbougle Dunes walk from the 4th green to the 5th tee along Bass Strait.

view, and it is stupefying. In full view is a crescent-shaped inlet with rolling surf and a wide beach with beautifully colored water. I do not say this lightly, but it is almost as good as the walk from the 14th green to the 15th tee at Cypress Point, which is the finest in golf. It is hard to say how excited we were after playing the 4th and 5th; they are a wondrous collection of back-to-back holes, as good as any stretch on any golf course. The 5th green is located near the 4th tee, and since we were the last group of the day and there was nobody behind us, we returned immediately to the 4th tee to play the holes again.

The next day we were in the Barnbougle clubhouse asking about the new course, Lost Farm, which had recently been seeded, but was not yet ready to play. The owner of the resort, Richard Sattler, came out from his office and offered to show us around.

Barnbougle Dunes, Tasmania, 4th green.

Sattler is a Tasmanian native—a burly local spud farmer and rancher, he is an unpretentious enigma. He was as excited as a kid on Christmas morning to show us his new toy. He drove us around the course in his beat up four-by-four on a rainy day and it was one of the highlights of my trip Down Under. If you ever become jaded by corporate-driven, cart-path only, waterfall-spectacle golf as an adjunct to real-estate development, come and spend some time with Richard Sattler. Playing golf should leave you in a sense of emotional renewal, and as we finally departed from Barnbougle we were immensely renewed indeed.

CHAPTER SIX

Playing the World's Elite Courses in an Earlier Era

The first part of this chapter will take a brief digression from looking at how to gain access to clubs today and will take a look back at an early obsessive globetrotting golf nut. I was curious to see how he was able to access some of his courses and how much traditions may have changed. He pursued his dream in the era of operator-assisted telephone calls, typewriters and carbon paper, and before ubiquitous air travel and golf course rankings.

Nicknamed "Red" for his strawberry blond hair, the five-foot-ten-inch Ralph Kennedy of New York was a founding member of Winged Foot. Ralph was featured in the *USGA Journal* in 1951 and they called him the "Dr. Livingstone of Golf." The USGA described Ralph as a "portly man of medium size with a jolly twinkle in his eyes." He gave up the game in 1953 due to poor eyesight, but not before playing 8,500 rounds over a forty-two-year period, which amounts to over 200 rounds a year; a tall feat. Not only was Ralph portly, but the man had stamina. He did this while holding down a full-time job as a traveling salesman for a pencil company. By the time of his death in 1961, he had played 3,150 distinct courses in fourteen countries.

Ralph was detail-oriented and kept every card from the courses he played. His nomadic journey is attested to because he had someone from each course sign his card, usually the pro or a superintendent. He donated all of them and his other memorabilia to the USGA, whose museum and library are located in Far Hills, New Jersey, an hour from my house. I thought I would go and have a look, to see what I could learn about how golf has changed over the last century and how he was able to access some of his courses.

Ralph gave himself the title of "The Peripatetic Golfer," and had it printed on the cover of each of his six thick scrapbooks. The definition of peripatetic: "Walking about or from place to place; traveling on foot," which is perhaps an understatement in Ralph's case. The USGA estimates that over his lifetime he walked two times the circumference of the earth—50,000 miles—playing golf.

In addition to his accomplishment playing so many golf courses, Ralph was a master of public relations. In total, there were over 500 different clippings from newspapers and magazines featuring him in his scrapbooks, and when stacked on top of one another they measure over a foot high. He was featured in *The New Yorker*, the *Chicago Daily News*, the *New York Sun*, the *Daily Mirror*, the *New York Evening Post,* the *New York Times,* and hundreds of other publications. Hand-drawn illustrations of him appeared twice on the cover of the *Saturday Evening Post.* He was a hoarder and his scrapbooks are filled with receipts from his golf trips, letters, and travel itineraries, along with loads of well-kept but brittle news-clippings.

The media began covering Kennedy in 1927 and they continued for another twenty-six years. Among the sports reporters with a keen interest in Ralph was O. B. Keeler of the *Atlanta Journal,* a well-regarded writer. Keeler was a friend of Bobby Jones and followed his career up close. Having Keeler write about you periodically during this period is today's equivalent of being featured regularly on ESPN or having Jim Nantz interview you every three months.

Ralph's long journey began in 1911 at the city-run Van Cortlandt Park Golf Course in the Bronx, and his original card is in the USGA library; scrawled across the top is "course #1." The best I could determine from his correspondence, the primary method he used to access courses was to leverage his membership at Winged Foot by writing to the course ahead of time or by carrying a "letter of introduction" from his professional. He played at some of the best in the country, including early on at Garden City (course No. 21 in 1916), Maidstone (course No. 605 in 1929), Chicago Golf Club (course No. 1,277 in 1934), and both the Cypress Point and San Francisco golf clubs (courses No.

The dapper Ralph Kennedy boarding his 1951 flight to Great Britain (*USGA Museum*).

2,501 and 2,508, respectively in 1946). His favorite course was Pine Valley (course No. 301 in 1926).

Prior to his 1951 trip to the British Isles, he solicited every letter of introduction possible. He received letters from the USGA, the president of Winged Foot, the Metropolitan Golf Association, and from *Golf Monthly Magazine* (Edinburgh), asking to be extended courtesies to play. While there for twenty-four days he played thirty-five courses including Muirfield, Gleneagles, North Berwick, Prestwick, Carnoustie, Sunningdale, Wentworth, Swinley Forest, Royal Dublin, and Portmarnock. He played the Old Course at St. Andrews as his 3,000th course and had the newly installed captain of the Royal & Ancient Golf Club sign his card. The new captain, who took office two days after Ralph played, was none other than Francis Ouimet, winner of the US Open at the Country Club in 1913 at the age of twenty. Ralph and I do share at least one trait; during his trip overseas a British reporter asked him about his hobby. His reply was, "It's no hobby, son. It's an obsession."

The headline writers coined many names for Ralph, including golf marathoner, golf nomad, itinerant golfer, pencil peddler, golf glutton, golf course collector, globetrotting golfer, champion rambler of golfdom, gallivanting golfer, link trotter, and a golfing Lou Gehrig.

His scrapbooks take you back in time; especially notable are the methods he used to communicate. A confirmation letter he received in 1935 notes that it is "confirming our telephonic conversation," as if it is a novelty. There are several classic Western Union telegrams in the scrapbooks with the ticker tape pasted onto them in all capital letters, as was the standard then. In the United States, Ralph traveled by bus, train, subway, taxi, and automobile, but he also sailed on ocean liners when traveling to South America and Bermuda. One of the more fascinating documents in the scrapbooks is an original "radiogram" message sent in 1930 by ship-to-shore transmission when he was off the coast of Panama, "Can Mr. Kennedy play golf in Gatun at 2.30 this afternoon." He did fly, only once, to the British Isles on his 1951 trip, out of Idlewild airport (today's John F. Kennedy International), but apparently was nervous about it. His last scrapbook contains a letter from his insurance company confirming that his policy has "no aviation restrictions whatsoever."

Ralph was able to play Augusta, and his card is thankfully in the USGA library where it belongs. He played it as course number 1,093 on April 22, 1933, which is one year before the first Masters. The card is a rarity because it is one of the few surviving cards showing the course in its original configuration. When Augusta opened the two sets of nine holes were reversed, and Ralph's card shows that. The front and back were flipped to today's configuration eighteen months later, in late 1934. There was no record of how he got on Augusta in his scrapbook—his was the only name on the scorecard—but the redheaded golfing sensation played the course three months after it officially opened, so my guess is he knew a founding member (Grantland Rice), or it is likely O. B. Keeler assisted. As if his card isn't rare enough, it was signed by P. J. A. Berckmans as superintendent; he was a member of the family that owned the Fruit-lands Nursery before Bobby Jones bought it to build the course. Berckmans assisted in the program to develop each of the holes of the course with different flowering plants and trees, including the removal of existing plants—including azaleas—from their original locations in the nursery to line the fairways. Berckmans was not only a green keeper but was also invited to be a member, a real rarity and something you would clearly never see today. Kennedy made notations on the card next to several holes, the only one of his cards I looked at where he did so. Next to No. 3—today's 12th—he wrote "most picturesque." On No. 4—today's 13th—he wrote "best long," and on No. 14—today's 5th—had the "sportiest green."

Red wasn't shy; among the letters in his last scrapbook was one from the White House. Ralph wrote to Eisenhower asking if they could play together. A secretary wrote back to Ralph, saying, "I am sorry, however, that we cannot give you any assurance that such a game as you suggest can be arranged. Frankly, the President's time for recreation is so limited that it is impossible to make any plans of this nature in advance." The last sentence isn't exactly true, as you will see shortly.

Ralph was featured in *National Geographic* in 1952 and discussed how hard the National Golf Links was to gain entry into. In the article they note, "Probably no course anywhere is more exclusive. Golfers from other clubs get no automatic playing privileges at the National." They continue, "Some think it is easier to get into the White House than into the National's club. Prospective candidates for membership

National Golf Links of America, Southampton, New York windmill.

may wait a decade or more to be admitted." Ralph played the National in 1929 as course number 605 and disclosed a little-known fact, that Eisenhower was an honorary member of the club. Ike genuinely earned his place in the World Golf Hall of Fame because *while president* he played over 900 rounds of golf, or over 100 rounds per year. I'm not sure how Ike's secretary was able to write to Ralph in 1953 with a straight face saying the commander in chief's recreation time was limited.

Ralph was a real trailblazer, and there is not enough room in this book to fully elaborate on his story. There is so much more to it, and it has whetted my appetite enough that I am planning a book about him telling his complete story. My own unorthodox story of playing the National Golf Links follows.

The Keeper of the Green

Of all the ways I was able to play the golf courses on my list, the story of how I got on two of the best is noteworthy. In addition to my other pursuits, and as someone who loves the game, I am an avid collector of golf books and sell them as an avocation. I have an online golf bookstore, issue a catalog, and trade with other collectors. During the Masters several years ago, I received a call from somebody who found my name on the website. "Hello, I'm a superintendent at Shinnecock Hills, how would you like to come out and play?" No question, I thought it was one of my friends playing a practical joke on me, so I started laughing. Shinnecock is a legendary golf course that even lay people know the name of: a founding-member club of the USGA, host to US Opens, and ranked as the fourth-best course in the world.

As I continued talking to the caller I concluded it was not a joke. He was a collector of golf books and we talked for half an hour. I was invited out and played, and the experience was worthy of Shinnecock's esteemed place in the golf world on all counts. A deceptive course, Shinnecock embodies the opposite of John Darby's design philosophy; the course "looks easy, plays hard," especially the par-3 7th and 11th holes, which are devilish.

Through multiple good turns of fortune, I have been lucky enough to play Shinnecock an additional five times through various means, but none beats the charmed first time I played it. I was scheduled to go out to Southampton one additional time to meet deep-throat and play again, this time with two friends from California, but the night before, he called and said he had bad news. The course was going to be closed, but, because he felt bad, he had arranged for us to play on the National Golf Links, which abuts Shinnecock.

The National Golf Links of America

If you knew me better, you would understand why I buy lottery tickets every week, because I have been very lucky my whole life and I figure it's only a matter of time.

National Golf Links of America clubhouse exterior view.

The National is not as well-known as Shinnecock, but it is one of the grand dames of American golf. In addition to what I have described about it thus far, the course is ranked in the top twenty-five in the world, every hole is patterned after a famous hole in the British Isles, and as Ralph Kennedy said, invitations to play are issued sparingly.

Playing at the National is a treat for the senses from the first tee until the last green. Among its eighteen equally good and unique holes the 16th—named "Punchbowl"—stands out as *primus inter pares,* first among equals. The par-4 plays up a rising hill with the iconic National windmill at the top, and its punchbowl green is one of the best in golf. When you finish putting out on the 16th you can't see much of anything except the sides of the punchbowl. It is noticeably quiet because you are sunken down into the landscape. Macdonald's philosophy about golf was that the primary purpose was to allow you to be alone with nature, and he achieved his goal here in spades. Standing in the splendid isolation of the punchbowl green, you feel as

National Golf Links "Punchbowl" 16th green approach.

if you are the only person on the planet. To proceed to the next tee you walk up the hill and at the apex you see the beautiful expanse of Peconic Bay out ahead of you; the windmill and clubhouse are on your left and the 17th hole is beneath you. The 17th is one of the great short par-4 risk-reward holes in the golf world—along with the 10th at Riviera. The shimmering bay sits behind the green. The fairway—presented elegantly below you—is sheer perfection. Playing at the National is exhilarating and makes the heart pump a little bit faster.

The National is famous for its lunch, which hasn't changed since the course opened. The staples of the lunch are locally caught lobster and also fish cakes, crab cakes, beef

The dining room at the National Golf Links of America.

and kidney pie, shepherd's pie, and macaroni and cheese, eaten in a majestic dining room overlooking the 18th green.

After playing the National for the first time, my playing partner and I tried to go into the clubhouse to take a look around, because I knew it was such a titillating place. Before I could even put my hand on the doorknob, the majordomo came out and asked if he could help us. I told him we wanted to take a quick look around, and he said we couldn't because we had golf shoes on. He was being polite. I said, *no problem*, we would be happy to go put on our street shoes, and he said—in the tone of an angry

National Golf Links of America Clubhouse.

headmaster—that we're not welcome, and we were thus rebuffed. I made a mental note to make sure one day I would return so I could see the interior.

Well, I was invited back a couple of times over the years by a member I eventually met. Two of the most memorable days in my entire life were ones I spent at the National, playing in a tournament of sixteen golfers. We stayed in the clubhouse overnight, in dormitory-style rooms on the top floor. We started with the famous lunch, played a round of golf, and then had cocktails outside. The scene was idyllic, with a gentle breeze blowing, enveloping us with the pleasant smell of the sea, while the sounds of nearby gulls filled the air. We had dinner in the long green-colored dining room and afterward sat in the library, which has an imposing picture of C. B. Macdonald above it. We played cards until the wee hours of the morning in the "green" room, and the following day enjoyed breakfast in the clubhouse, followed by another round of golf. Spending a day at the National makes you feel as if you are golfing royalty; it's as good as it gets.

To emphasize the exclusivity of the club, a good story in *Legendary Golf Clubs of the American East* tells how Tom Watson called the club one day as he was preparing to play in the US Open at Shinnecock Hills next door. He wanted to come over with Ben Crenshaw and Greg Norman but was told he could not play because he was not a member. After he was turned away he thought about it, called back in a couple of minutes, and asked if there was any way he could be introduced to a member so they could play. He was introduced and the lucky member played with the above named threesome.

A Perfect Score

As I have mentioned, there have only been thirty people who have accomplished the feat of playing the top 100 golf courses in the world, a number roughly equivalent to the number of men who have been to the moon. Most of the stories are interesting and some are unique, especially the journey of Samm Klaparda, the only woman who has succeeded in doing so. The task is particularly difficult for a woman since some of the golf clubs do not welcome members of the fairer sex as much as they do men. Case in point, Garden City Men's, which is all-male and doesn't openly welcome women. I've heard all kinds of apocryphal stories about how members' wives aren't even allowed to drive into the parking lot. Truth be told, women can play on a Monday or at the discretion of the club's executive committee, which apparently she did.

The most ambitious tale, though, is that of Robert McCoy, the second person to complete the grand quest. I described myself early on as being goal-oriented and prefer to plan everything out in advance. Well, I ain't got nothin' on Bob McCoy. Not satisfied with playing all top 100 courses once, when he was done he experienced a letdown, as I did. You see, playing all these courses and having a lofty goal produces adrenaline. It's analogous to getting hooked on a drug and you want it to continue. After you achieve the goal, at some level it is anticlimactic—although quite a nice problem to have. So Bob set another goal for himself. Why not play the top 100 courses again in 100 consecutive days? Now that would be a stretch. I have seen the spreadsheet Bob put together and his travel itinerary, and it is beautiful. Clearly McCoy has some of the best contacts in the golf world to be able to schedule and play courses when he wanted to, particularly Augusta. Bob pulled off the 100-in-100 feat in 1997, and in my view, it ranks right up there with the greatest accomplishments in the world of non-tournament golf.

We have come a long way from Ralph Kennedy's turbo-prop B.O.A.C. flight that would have taken him eleven hours to fly to Britain in 1951. McCoy did his round-the-world trip flying regularly scheduled commercial aviation and didn't miss any connections or have any flights delayed, and no weather interfered with his golf. The probability of all that happening smoothly is very low, and kudos to him for having the staying power to do it. Bob has promised to write a book about the experience and will tell all the details, so I do not want to spoil his story. Suffice it to say, I will be one of the first people to buy his book.

SECTION II
The Difficult Courses and Advanced Methods

CHAPTER SEVEN
The More Difficult to Access United States Courses and Clubs

Thus far I have delved into the easier courses and some of the more difficult ones, and I have looked at how to play many of the greatest courses outside the United States that are welcoming if you follow their rules. In this chapter and subsequent chapters we lay out some of the more advanced ways to gain access and look at how I managed invitations from some very difficult to play clubs, including, ultimately, Augusta National.

Career Choices

The first two methods outlined are tongue-in-cheek, because they are more life choices than anything else, although worth spending a little time on. One of the best ways to connect into this world is to choose the right career. As I have said, working in the financial world was a huge advantage to me, particularly working at a firm that had a history of being golf obsessed, with several former chairmen who were or are members of Augusta.

So, you are coming out of Stanford Business School and have your choice of jobs. What do you do? Go to Silicon Valley and try to change the world, or do you enter the world of Wall Street? If you have an interest in golf and want to work around the clock, then Wall Street it is. The best firms to work at for networking purposes are Morgan Stanley, Merrill Lynch, J. P. Morgan, or the boutique investment banks such as Sandler O'Neill, Keefe, Bruyette & Woods, or Allen & Company. Or, a host of private equity or hedge funds who have partners or owners who are über-golfers. If numbers are not your thing, but you like to travel and tell people what to do, then the strategy firms are a good career choice. Working at McKinsey & Company, Bain & Co., or Boston Consulting Group will likely provide all the connections you need to access the crème de la crème of courses.

Likewise, if you are younger still and are deciding where to go to college, it could be a chance to get into some cloistered clubs. To give two examples, the Harvard golf team has access to the Country Club at Brookline, and the UCLA team practices at ten clubs in the LA area including the Los Angeles Country Club, Riviera, Bel-Air, and the Lakeside Golf Club of Hollywood. Talk about having the world as your oyster at a young age, these kids are living the dream. If anyone has ever told you that life was fair, you need to look no further than the privileges these students receive to know they were lying.

An additional method to gain access to one of the best courses in the world is to attend Yale. If that is not in your future, then knowing a student, alumnus, or faculty member will also get the job done. The Course at Yale, located in New Haven, is a classic Macdonald-Raynor design that allows non-members to play if you are introduced by any of the above.

If your career is already established, all is not lost. We'll come back later to another good method to find a way onto the courses you want, but first we'll dive into a below-the-radar place that represents the apex of the club world.

The Links

As you have seen, one of the best ways to gain access to clubs is to connect with the right people who are members of the most prestigious clubs. One such club has a good pedigree and strong associations to the world of golf, although it has no golf course. I have included it for reasons that will soon be obvious, and it is clearly one of the most

The Links, New York City.

elite in the world of golf. It functions as a social and eating club and is located on 36 East Sixty-Second Street in New York City, between Madison and Park Avenues. It is called The Links. Not The Links Club, simply The Links.

The Links was founded by Charles Blair Macdonald and his friends in 1916. The objectives of The Links are "to promote and conserve throughout the United States the best interests and true spirit of the game of golf as embodied in its ancient and honorable traditions, endorsing the rules of the game as it is played in Scotland and as adopted by the Royal & Ancient Golf Club of St. Andrews." Although it has no actual course, its members are some of the most connected in the world of golf.

The club is housed in a stunning four-story Georgian town house with a mansard roof, which was built in 1890. The *Architectural Record* described the club in 1917 as showing "the effects of quiet breeding, traditional elegance, of considered good taste." A discreet club, there is no sign announcing that the building houses The Links; there is no grand entrance and no imposing staircase outside. In fact, I walked right past it on my first attempt to find it. A small stairway leads you down to an entry door located below street level; then you enter through a set of double doors. As you open the first door and close it behind you, you enter a small vestibule; you then open another door and enter this private sanctuary. It is as if standing between the two doors transports you to a different world. In my imagination, it is the equivalent of going through the transporter on *Star Trek*, being beamed to another planet, or, if you are from a younger generation, it feels as if you have been transported to Hogwarts in *Harry Potter*. The world you have entered into is very dignified.

Midtown Manhattan is home to many private social clubs, among them, the Grolier, Lotos, Union League, Union, Lambs, Metropolitan, Yale, Harvard, Century, Cornell, Princeton, Colony, Knickerbocker, Cosmopolitan, Vassar, University, Harmonie, Brook, and of course The Links. Each club was founded with a different constituency in mind. Some are for those in the arts and literary world, others for alumni; The Links having been formed by and for prosperous golfers. While New York City is probably the most meritocratic city in the world, it has a whole host of these private social clubs most people never see.

As you enter, you are greeted by a serious-looking gentleman wearing a smart-looking green jacket with black lapels and a "links man" logo on the sleeve. All the employees wear this sharp uniform, many with a bowtie. Aside from Augusta, if there were a place in the golf world where they would actually take your ticket and punch it as a badge to show you have arrived, this is it. Unfortunately, I forgot to bring my ticket with me so the manager gave me a skeptical glare, the type with the brow raised a little that says, "You don't belong here, do you?" Fortunately, I was wearing the requisite jacket and tie and pronounced the member's name right, so he let me stay.

Macdonald's founding members were the powerful and successful of New York during his era. They included Charles H. Sabin (president of Guaranty Trust, the forerunner to today's J. P. Morgan and an early Augusta member), Harry Payne Whitney (a sportsman and man of leisure), James Stillman (president of National City Bank, the predecessor of today's Citibank), William C. Potter (a future president of Guaranty Trust), and Frank L. Crocker (a prominent attorney). The Links was started because a friend of C. B. Macdonald's wasn't admitted into the Brook, so Macdonald quit that club and started The Links as a place where those that played at Shinnecock and the National could meet in the city.

It is a USGA type-two sanctioned club. Although not widely known, the USGA does not require a club to have a course. The requirement is merely that you must have a reasonable and regular opportunity for members to play golf with each other. Given its historic founding, the USGA regularly holds an annual dinner at The Links, and the current president of the USGA is given an honorary membership during their tenure.

The Links is the archetypal private club. After you go through the double doors you are in the entrance lobby, and on a cold and gray day the fireplace will likely be crackling to provide a warm welcome. In the rear of the building on the first floor is a private dining room, the Oak Room. Standing in the entry foyer, your eye is immediately drawn to the centerpiece of the building, the green oval spiral staircase adorned with a wrought-iron railing. The staircase runs the height of the town house, from the first floor to the fourth. Throughout the club there is architectural detailing that gives The Links its remarkable qualities, including decorative trim along the outside of the staircase as it spins upward in a counter clockwise fashion. The manager of the club stands behind a wooden, glass-topped built-in counter which holds a treasure trove of items adorned with The Links logo, such as ties, shirts, playing cards, and the club history book. My first time there I made my usual forthright inquiry if any were available for purchase, and was snubbed with alacrity.

The second floor is the club's *pièce de résistance*. The front of the building contains the Sir Christopher Wren room, which serves as the library. The paneling was brought over from England, from a room designed by Sir Christopher Wren. There is sufficiently high-quality artwork hanging in the club that if it were not private, it could serve as a museum or gallery. For example, in the library is a Rembrandt Peale portrait of George Washington, flanked by iconic portraits of Abraham Lincoln and Captain James Lawrence, the famous American naval officer who is known for his dying command, "Don't give up the ship."

The library has clusters of leather chairs and sofas spread around; in each cluster is a discreet buzzer button, should you require service. The room also has two little writing tables with inkwells and a selection of high quality Links stationery and envelopes, should you need to dash off a quick note. The club doesn't acknowledge the fact that people no longer sit down at writing tables and send little notes in our modern era of instant messaging and cell phones. Being somewhat of a Luddite myself, though, I am drawn to it. Located at the far end of the room is a large table that holds various golf and sporting books and magazines including *Yale Alumni Magazine, Harvard Magazine*, and most importantly, lest we forget where we are, there are copies of the last three years *Social Register,* easily accessible, should the need arise to check someone's pedigree on short notice.

In the rear of the building on the second floor is the C. B. Macdonald room, which is dominated by an original life-size painting of Macdonald above the fireplace, standing with a caddie, with the National Golf Links windmill in the background. He is wearing plus fours and surveying the room below. The painting was commissioned by and presented to the club by industrialist and Carnegie Steel chairman Henry C. Frick.

In between the library and the C. B. Macdonald room is the bar area and my favorite part of the club, one of the most idiosyncratic places I have ever been in. Above the bar is a large painting of *The First Meeting of the North Berwick Golf Club* (painted in 1833), a treasured work of golf art. The bar has dark woods and extensive paneling; it has several little notched-out areas and a small corridor lined with

Picture in The Links bar area, *The First Meeting of the North Berwick Golf Club* (*North Berwick, Scotland*).

oak-paneled liquor lockers, each about two-feet by two-feet in size. In the back of the bar area down a narrow corridor is a snug little area that has leather bench seating. Crammed into this small space is a leather backgammon table and above are three skylights. It is dark, intimate, and cozy in a way you would imagine a premier men's club would be, although The Links now admits female members. It is not hard to imagine Links members sitting in here during Prohibition drinking their private stashes and smoking cigars.

The third floor contains the dining room in the front of the building, and above the fireplace is a painting of one-time member Dwight D. Eisenhower wearing his Links patterned tie. The fireplace is decorated with original eighteenth-century Dutch delft golfing tiles, which were the inspiration to Macdonald for the "links man" logo, the same one that adorns the National Golf Links logo. Sitting in the dining room is an experience; it seemed to me the room had the highest concentration of Hermès ties per capita in the world. Although I felt welcome at The Links, when my host visited the men's room during lunch, I was under the distinct impression the waiting staff were keeping an extra close eye on me, for fear I might take some of the monogrammed tableware if left unattended.

Although I have digressed into a long look at the feel of the club, the purpose of including it here is because it has such tight linkages into the golf world, it is an exceptional place to make connections should you ever meet a member. The club holds events each year at various golf courses. To give you a sample of the quality of golf we are talking about, I noticed on the bulletin board a list of the successful events the club held the prior year; included on the list were events at Shinnecock Hills, Maidstone, Fishers Island, the National Golf Links, the Chicago Golf Club, Deepdale, and Somerset Hills.

The Links has 1,000 members, 500 of whom are non-resident, consistent with its national charter, and membership is by invitation only. I looked through the current membership directory while there and on page thirty-three alone recognized the names of three well-known current or ex-CEOs. Out of respect for their privacy and because I'm not stupid and want to be invited back, I won't publish the names of the members, but it is a tempting thought. Suffice it to say, similar to the founding members, they remain well-heeled and connected.

As I was sitting in the bar talking about the club, its tradition, and its membership rules, the board-certified WASP who was my host mentioned it takes five members to sponsor a new member. Our conversation was going well and he asked what clubs I was a member of. Note the presumption in the plural nature of the question, it is assumed you are a member of multiple clubs. I sensed an opening; that if, perhaps, I was affiliated with some good clubs, maybe he was considering sponsoring me. This would be the ultimate coup for me. When I mentioned I am a member of Sam's Club, the Hair Club for Men, and the mile-high club, I saw the blue blood drain out of his face.

In my research I found a membership handbook for the club from 1955, and it gives a good sense of how much power was amassed within the walls of this small town house in Manhattan, thirty-nine years after its founding. The sitting commander-in-chief, Dwight Eisenhower, and Augusta cofounder Cliff Roberts were members, as was the current and prior president and secretary of the United States Golf Association. Cypress Point cofounder Roger D. Lapham was a member, as was Eugene Homans, who Bobby Jones defeated at Merion in the 1930 U. S. Amateur to complete the Grand Slam.

Flipping through page after page was a list of power brokers extraordinaire. Imagine walking into the bar and seeing Bill Boeing, Eddie Rickenbacker, Jimmy Doolittle, and Lucius Clay bantering back and forth about aviation. Or wander into the library and talk investments with the *actual* Morgan, his partner Stanley, and Dean Witter himself. Or discuss our military strategy with the current secretaries of the Navy and Air Force, as well as a future secretary of defense. If politics is your calling, you're in luck, with a pair of US senators, a future secretary of state, a governor, and a big-city mayor perhaps having a smoke in the game room. Happen to be an Anglophile? Then discuss Great Britain with the current, former, and future US ambassadors to the Court of St. James's, all three of whom were members in 1955. If trust-fund babies are your thing, look around the C. B. Macdonald Room and you might spot heirs to the fortunes of McGraw Hill, Mellon Bank, the Sun Oil Company, and the Marshall Field department store sipping their cocktails. Perhaps it is no coincidence that an astounding twenty-four members of the 1955 Links have been featured on the cover of *Time Mag-*

azine, since its publisher, Henry Luce, was also listed as a member. Round it out with the chairman of AT&T, US Steel, Shell Oil, General Foods, Nabisco, Georgia Pacific, Texaco, Ford Motor, Proctor & Gamble, IBM, General Electric, Standard Oil, Merck, and the CEOs of a dozen large banks. Ike's definition of the "military-industrial" complex can neatly be summed up by the membership of The Links in 1955.

One always has a keen sense of where you are in the social hierarchy when at The Links, and it is clear you are at the pinnacle; as their club history describes it, it is "ageless . . . old-fashioned . . . timeless." My advice is be on the lookout for anyone you meet wearing a tie with a little green links man on it, because they likely can help you gain entry into some ritzy golf courses.

Clubs without Courses

I briefly covered golfing societies in an earlier chapter as a good way to make connections with others that love the game. And, as you have seen with The Links, superior connections are to be made at clubs without their own courses. An extension of this is a couple of "national" or "international" golfing society clubs. In the United States the most prominent one is called the Outpost Club, based out of Toledo, established a couple of years ago by avid golfers. The Outpost Club hosts over fifty events a year at various clubs around the United States and they are almost universally at premier ones. A review of a recent year's list of outings included play at the Olympic Club, East Lake, Piping Rock in Long Island, Oakland Hills in Michigan, Muirfield Village in Ohio, and Oakmont. The club has raised over $250,000 since its founding to support charity, including an event at the super-exclusive Deepdale on Long Island, reputedly the club with the most billionaire members in the United States. Of course, there is a fee to join the club, there are annual dues, and fees to play in its events, but given the access they are providing and the contacts you will make, it is ideally suited to itinerant golf nuts. The Outpost has some home clubs they grant members access to, as does the Eden Club, which is a similar type of club with an international twist. The Eden Club is based in St. Andrews, Scotland, and offers access to courses there, and they also host events at some of the finest clubs in the world including Riviera and Sebonack. In addition, they have their own historic baronial castle, Pittormie, which was formerly the home of the Duke of Fife. Joining both clubs is by invitation only and you can visit their respective websites for more details.

Corporate Membership

One potentially overlooked method to playing at a club you want is to see if you can leverage a corporate membership. Many corporations have memberships that they use to entertain clients. Even if you think you might not have the best contacts, think about people you are working with or know who aren't even necessarily golfers and find out if the company they work for has a membership. I used this method to access two courses, and the one most likely to work for a broad group of people is East Lake, which is a revered place in the world of golf. The interior of the clubhouse is a shrine to Bobby Jones and it includes his Calamity Jane putter, the original scroll conferring the 1958 Freedom of the Burgh of St. Andrews on him, his hickory shafted clubs, and his original lockers. It includes full-size replicas of all four of his Grand Slam trophies from 1930, which is fitting, because it was at East Lake all four were together in one place.

Today the course is owned and run by the East Lake Foundation, a local non-profit whose mission is to give back to the East Lake neighborhood, which it has been instrumental in reviving. Tom Cousins was the driving force behind this unorthodox structure. He purchased the course in 1993, invested $25 million, and donated it to the foundation. Their mission, "Golf with a Purpose," is supported by corporations from around the country, who are the primary members.

Leveraging the Course Architect

Non-golfers can recognize certain golf courses such as Pebble Beach and the Old Course at St. Andrews by name. I remember when I first received my "peg" board, looking at it and being surprised at the number-eleven ranked course in the world by the name of Sand Hills, located in, of all places, Mullen, Nebraska. As a private course located far from home, I didn't have a good way to find a member. Sand Hills has only 150–160 members who are scattered all over, and the course is only open for their short playing season in the summer. I have never met anyone in the New York metropolitan area who knows a member, and getting onto Sand Hills proved a challenge. The normal ways of finding a member I used for other courses didn't work, so I resorted to an unusual method. The golf course was designed by the Texas based team of Bill Coore and Ben Crenshaw. One of my golfing companions knew someone who knew Bill and he was able to set us up to play unaccompanied, something the course permits once if you know a member (or, apparently, gladly, the architect as well).

Expectations were high going into my trip to Sand Hills. How could a course built in 1995 rank higher than Merion, Ballybunion, Carnoustie, and Riviera, to name a few?

My view of the United States is more or less consistent with the famous *The New Yorker* cartoon. The country consists of New York, some other East Coast cities, New Jersey, and California. Nebraska is part of the vast Midwest that I give little thought to; flyover country. Why in the world would anyone want to go to Nebraska? The only people I know who go there attend Warren Buffet's annual shareholder meeting in Omaha.

Well, I have to tell you, this view of Nebraska was shattered for me by going there once. The Sand Hills region is out of this world. It is not the row-after-row of cornfields and flatlands I imagined; to the contrary, it is one of the natural wonders of this country. My trip to Sand Hills began with a flight into Denver, which is the closest large city to Mullen, and is a five-and-a-half-hour drive at that. The overall journey to Sand Hills took me longer than many of my trips to play in Britain and Ireland. You can also fly to Sand Hills by taking a commuter flight from either Denver or Chicago into North Platte, Nebraska, which is about an hour from the course, but, with afternoon thunderstorms common in this part of the country, I opted to drive. For the investment bankers, hedge fund managers, and private equity readers out there, the good news is you will be able to land your private jets in North Platte, although if you do, you are missing one of the memorable parts of Sand Hills, which is the journey there.

After leaving Denver, we took Interstate 76 through a part of Northern Colorado that is bland and nondescript, a high plain with mile after mile of scrub. Crossing into Nebraska, it is essentially more of the same until about three hours into the trip when you hit Nebraska State Highway 61. The contrast to the area you have traveled through is striking. NE-61 is one of the hidden gem, sleeper roads of this country; for beauty, it rivals driving between San Francisco and Los Angeles on US-1 along the coast, although it is a stark and subtle beauty that reveals itself slowly. I had no idea what the Sand Hills region even was prior to this trip. I assumed there was a small area of dunes where they built a good golf course. The reality is the Sand Hills region is 19,300-square miles and takes up about 25 percent of the entire landmass of the state. This is larger than the states of Connecticut, New Jersey, Delaware, and Rhode Island combined. A geological anomaly, the Sand Hills region was formed at the end of the last ice age, when sand was windblown into large dunes during a severe drought. It has some of the biggest sand dunes I have seen anywhere in the world, some over 300 feet tall, meaning it must have been one hell of a drought.

Driving along NE-61 rounding bend after bend, your mind starts to play tricks on you. You will look away and look back, and think once you travel over the crest of the next hill you might see the Atlantic Ocean or the Irish Sea. The beauty of the region is unexpected; it is bucolic, peaceful, and dramatic as you drive along rolling hills punctuated by occasional ranches. To call the area sparsely populated is an understatement. The county seat in Arthur we drove through had a post office, bank, county courthouse, a fairground, and not much else. The total population of the *county* Sand Hills is located in is less than 750 people. There are more people than that on one subway train during my morning commute.

I felt at times I was in a time warp—in many of the places I drove through it could have been 1930. The drive on NE-61 is for a full hour, which is a good thing, because the anticipation builds the more you drive. It is a right turn onto NE-2 to make the final approach into Mullen; once you enter into Mullen (population 509, and yes, those are bullet holes in the road sign), you make an additional right onto NE-97 south. The club will have previously told you to look for mile marker 55 on the left side of the road, and the golf club is your next right. Once you turn off the road, it is two and a half miles to the clubhouse. The clubhouse is a decidedly understated affair, as are the guest cabins, which sleep two and are set on the top of a hill overlooking the Dismal River. You never receive a key since the cabins are on the honor system and are unlocked. The booklet left in each room for guests warns you not to be alarmed if you hear strange sounds in the night, since deer often bed down under the cabins and wild turkeys are known to roost on the porch railings.

The Golf Course at Sand Hills

Did the course live up to its number-eleven world ranking? Yes. It deserves to be ranked among the best in the world even though it was built relatively recently. The golf course has *no* weak holes, which, aside from Pine Valley, Cypress Point, and the National Golf Links, is hard to say about almost any course in the world. The land was destined for

Sand Hills Golf Club, Mullen, Nebraska.

golf, and architects Coore & Crenshaw did a masterful job designing the course. In 1993, they visited the site and "discovered" over 130 golf holes, and then proceeded to narrow it down to only eighteen, which is the golf course the world is lucky to have today. Although the area is windy, there is no prevailing wind, so the course is routed to be playable in any wind condition. I'm not sure how you design a course as good as Coore & Crenshaw did, but they pulled it off.

I have never met Dick Youngscap, the owner and driving force behind Sand Hills, but the man is an obvious visionary. With the possible exception of Mike Keiser and Bandon Dunes, no one has had greater vision in sponsoring and developing a golf course since Charles Blair Macdonald, when he built the National Golf Links in 1911. The entire club is on 8,000 acres of land. By way of comparison, the East Course at Merion was built on only 120 acres.

The golf course is located one mile from the clubhouse over sand dunes; you drive out from the clubhouse in a golf cart, across a private ranch, and then arrive at the small starter's cabin and outdoor grill room nicknamed Ben's Porch. Part of what makes the course shine is that every green except the 17th is accessible from the front, encouraging bump and run or pitch shots, and the fairways blend into the greens in a spectacular fashion. Many holes play uphill so you can frequently misjudge and under-club, in which case you are going to be hitting a similar shot again, with the ball rolling back to your feet on pitch shots in shades of Pinehurst No. 2. Because of the shifting winds the holes on the course are not handicap rated, which makes for unorthodox match play because you do not know where to give strokes.

Play is limited to fifty rounds a day, making it a real treat, and because there are so few golfers, it gives you the ability to go directly from the 18th green back to the 1st tee, should you so desire. While there, we did so desire, and did it more than once, the place is that brilliant. At times when playing Sand Hills it had the feel of Shinnecock Hills or other courses near the water. Many of the holes also have the feel of desert golf with wide fairways and "target" tee shots. Consistent with Coore & Crenshaw's design philosophy, it is the shots into the green you have to play well to post a good score at Sand Hills, and you have to putt well. To give you a sense of how few rounds a day are played here, it is roughly two groups an hour, or slightly more than Cypress Point, which has only forty

8th hole, Sand Hills, Nebraska.

rounds a day. By way of comparison, a typical course has about 150 rounds, sometimes many more.

I had a peaceful experience at Sand Hills and enjoyed the quiet beauty of the place. We stayed in cabin number fourteen, which sits on a bluff overlooking the Dismal River, and had coffee delivered to our cabin early each morning. Each cabin has a wooden deck on the back with wooden rocking chairs, and as the sun was coming up we enjoyed fresh-brewed coffee while listening to the sounds of the water running below. It was a total state of serenity and we saw no planes flying overhead and there was no background din of a distant highway. If you stop talking and listen, you will hear total silence punctuated only by the occasional bird chirping or wind blowing. The entire time at Sand Hills you are incommunicado, since there is basically no cell phone service, BlackBerries do not work, there is no wireless Internet connection, and there are no newspapers. The phones in your room will only let you make collect calls; it is a forced state of restful isolation, and let's hope they always keep it that way.

There are few places in the world left where you can still find true peace. In today's frenetic world we need to treasure places such as Sand Hills where you can still be completely at peace, can see the stars in the sky at night, disconnect from modern life, and enjoy the fresh air and wide-open spaces. Visiting Sand Hills reminded me that peace and quiet are to be treasured and that modern life is sometimes sadly out of balance. My journey there was much more than a trip to play golf; it was a life-changing experience, which is one of the unexpected lessons I learned pursuing my dream and what makes Sand Hills such a sought-after destination. If you are ever invited to play, you would be crazy to decline.

Special Experiences

Among the joyous aspects of golf are the intimate experiences you have playing where the greats have played before you. You can't go onto the field at Fenway Park, nor can you ride a horse down the stretch at Saratoga; but you can drop a ball on Merion's 18th fairway next to the Ben Hogan plaque and try to hit the green (not with a 1-iron). You can't drive in a Formula One race, but you can stand in the spot where Seve hit his shot from the parking lot at Lytham & St. Annes to win the 1979 Open Championship and be inspired.

My journey has been about so much more than playing the courses; it has been about experiencing the history of the game, the people I have met, and seeing some of the most stirring scenery in the world. And, about taking in each club's personality and unique style. Visiting them gives you a tantalizing glimpse into a different, refined world and allows you to truly appreciate and experience some of the best the world has to offer, which is why people become attracted to it. As a way to illustrate the point I will delve into some of the private courses of California as a microcosm of the phenomenon. All three featured below are among the hardest to penetrate and I was able to play them by eventually being introduced to a member who invited me. I tried some of the other methods outlined but they didn't work because these are so elite. Sorry, I have no silver bullet.

The Bel-Air Country Club

The West Side of Los Angeles is unlike any other place in America. The amount of wealth in Beverly Hills, Bel-Air, Century City, Holmby Hills, Westwood, Brentwood, Pacific Palisades, and the other neighborhoods is stunning. Bel-Air is the epicenter of this "La-La Land" and its members lead a charmed life. Designed by George Thomas Jr., Bel-Air is routed through four canyons and weaves its way in and out of them masterfully. The property has the feel of a massive Zen garden with the manicuring of the course, the structure and beauty of the trees, and the overall harmony of the place. Of course, it helps that every day of the year is seventy degrees with no humidity and that the light in

Swinging Bridge, 10th hole, Bel-Air Country Club.

Los Angeles is beautiful. To cross one canyon near the 10th hole, you walk across a large white swinging bridge. The experience of sitting inside their sprawling clubhouse after the round and hearing all the stories of what famous Hollywood types have done at Bel-Air, and spying some of the rich and famous in their own playground, is illuminating.

The Los Angeles Country Club

Not far from Bel-Air is the Los Angeles Country Club (LACC), which has another George Thomas Jr. designed course, the North—one of the best in the world. The club

Los Angeles Country Club, "little 17," North Course.

is an oasis within one of the largest and most densely populated urban areas in the country and sits on one of the most valuable pieces of land in the world. The southern boundary of the course is Santa Monica Boulevard. Wilshire Boulevard divides the North Course from the South, and Sunset Boulevard forms the rough northern boundary of the property. Having to pass through a guard gate to enter adds to the feeling of exclusivity. The club has many facets that make it noteworthy; when I visited the first time they set me up with a locker that was formerly Ronald Reagan's. Off the 13th green of the North course is the Playboy Mansion, and Aaron Spelling's 56,000 square-foot former chateau-style mansion is adjacent to the 14th.

To give you a sense of how exclusive LACC is, like at The Links Club, it is not possible to buy something from the pro shop because it only sells to members. My two visits to LACC have been among the most memorable and truly enjoyable in all my travels. Even if for a day, being able to visit the club and play the course, it gives you a sense of how the other half lives. Maybe I am a paparazzi at heart and easily impressed, or I like to gawk, but I do enjoy looking behind the scenes at these private clubs, to see what they are like, and to understand their culture. Some people spend their vacations in Los Angeles going to the Hard Rock Cafe, walking down the Hollywood Walk of Fame, or visiting a movie studio, which only allows you to experience it from the outside. These private clubs allow you to see the city from an insider's point of view and permit a small peek behind the veil.

The Cypress Point Club

In my view, the Cypress Point Club, located down the road from Pebble Beach, is the best golf course in the world. An Alister MacKenzie masterpiece, it has an unbeatable combination of factors that make it the best. This includes the genius of the routing, the uniqueness of the cypress trees, the artfulness of the bunkers, the bright-white sand, the color of the water in the bay, the ingeniousness of how MacKenzie camouflaged the traps, and the unbeatable views.

Herbert Warren Wind wrote about Cypress Point when they hosted the Walker Cup in 1981, "It should be emphasized that Cypress Point possesses a diversity of terrain possibly unmatched by any other course. It offers not only an unforgettable stretch of cliff-lined holes but some excellent orthodox seaside holes, a few stunning dune-land holes and an arresting sequence of holes that climb inland into hilly terrain, their fairways cut through a forest of Monterey pines. Back in 1929, Bobby Jones, who had come to California to play in the U. S. Amateur at Pebble Beach, found the time to get in two rounds at the newly-opened Cypress Point layout. Asked what he thought of the two courses, Jones, with his usual acumen and diplomacy, replied, 'Pebble Beach is more difficult, but Cypress Point is more fun.'"

If I had to classify Cypress Point as if it were a person, I would describe it as being the "complete package." It has good bones, stunning good looks, a charming personality, and it has aged gracefully. Most people know about the dramatic par-3 16th that plays over water; it is one of the most recognizable and photographed holes in golf.

Cypress Point, par-3 15th hole.

What most people may not realize is the other seventeen holes are equally as good. The hole before, the short 135-yard par-3 15th is the sexiest hole in golf, set in a secluded rocky cove with waves splashing all around it. Selwyn Herson, who completed playing the top 100 in 2004, summed up Cypress Point to *Travel & Leisure Golf* precisely in one sentence: "Playing in heaven: Six holes in the trees, six holes in the sand dunes, six holes by the sea."

If you are ever talking golf with someone who has played the course and they do not think Cypress Point ranks as one of the top three golf courses in the world, quietly take the scissors and letter opener off their desks, since they are clearly disturbed and

Cypress Point, 17th hole.

you are in danger; they belong in one of those white jackets with the crossing sleeves in front. For those golfers who aren't as pathological as I am and want to set a more modest goal than playing the top 100 courses in the world, I offer simple advice. Try to play Cypress Point. It encompasses all that is great in the world's golf courses into eighteen holes. It has an aura about it that almost no other course or club has, which makes it the zenith of a golfer's experience.

CHAPTER EIGHT

Gaining Access to Difficult Clubs Outside the United States

By now you should have an in-depth understanding of the myriad of ways to get invited to even the most cloistered clubs and have seen how it is possible to play some of the best golf in the world. Some of the hardest invitations to secure—aside from that impossible Georgia course—are courses outside our shores that do not openly welcome guests. This chapter delves into two of my toughest challenges.

Golf de Morfontaine

While everyone knows Augusta is the most difficult course to get onto, one below the radar for those focused outside the United States is Golf de Morfontaine, located in Senlis, France, a suburb of Paris, not far from Charles de Gaulle airport. Golf de Morfontaine was ranked as the forty-seventh best course in the world when I was trying to play it.

Early on, when I looked at the list of courses I wanted to play, I put them in a spreadsheet and broke them down into various categories: "easy to get on," "possible," "difficult," and "no clue." The private courses in Japan fell into the "no clue" category, as did several private United States courses I did not have even the remotest contact at. Morfontaine was also categorized this way.

Morfontaine was the brainchild of a member of the French aristocracy, the Duc de Gramont. In the interest of historical accuracy, since there have been fourteen holders of the title since 1643, specifically, it was the twelfth Duc, Antoine Agénor Armand de Gramont, who lived from 1879 until 1962. The Duc was a keen golfer and wanted a world-class course near his estate, Château de Valliére.

Morfontaine has a reputation as being a very private club, or, as they say in the native tongue: *club privé exclusivement réservé aux membres.* I had heard interesting stories about Morfontaine, although at the time I was attempting to gain access to it there was little public information available. It was designed by Tom Simpson, whose other courses I admire—namely Cruden Bay in Scotland and Ballybunion in Ireland—so I thought this would be a good one to attempt to play sooner rather than later.

Finding information about Golf de Morfontaine was not an easy task. I was able to obtain a picture of the clubhouse and brief descriptions in several books, but at the time the club had no website and no email address. Google Maps was gaining traction so I looked online and found a picture of the course from satellite and could see Morfontaine had twenty-seven holes.

I was able to locate the club's phone number, so I figured I would call them and see if they would let me come and play. Mind you, this is not a completely irrational thought. After all, even such esteemed European courses such as Muirfield and Royal County Down will take your call, respond to your email, and explain their booking procedures. Since I do not speak French, I had a French speaking female associate call on my behalf, to see if I could politely book a tee time. We wanted to approach them with the utmost respect, which we did, and I was completely flexible as to the date and time I was available to play.

Let's say her inquiries were met with what can best be described as a chilly reception. I'm not sure of the exact English translation of what they told her; however, I can't print it here and it's the rough equivalent of Marie Antoinette's, "let them eat cake." I was somewhat put off, because this stance is so much at odds with the founding tenets of the French Republic: *liberté, égalité, fraternité.* After all, all the world's golfers share a *fraternité*, do they not?

Not easily put off, I thought I would enlist the help of the American Embassy in Paris. This one I could do myself since they speak English. Morfontaine has had a long tradition of offering the current US Ambassador a membership so they could play golf in the spirit of good relations. I'm not sure whether the tradition continues to this day, but I thought it was worth a shot. The ambassador would not take my call and I was transferred to the American Citizen Services Office of the Consular section, which provides information and assistance to United States citizens. While the gentleman that took my call didn't tell me where to go directly, he made it clear he could be of no assistance.

Striking out on the first two attempts confirmed this one was going to be difficult. How exactly do you find a member of Morfontaine? I forged ahead with some creative attempts to gain access.

I thought long and hard, who is the most famous of French golfers? It is Arnaud Massy, who was the only Frenchman to win the Open Championship, in 1907 at Hoylake. Sadly, though, Arnaud died in 1950. Actually, the most well-known French golfer alive is our infamous friend Jean Van de Velde, who was almost the second Frenchman to win the Open Championship. *Bien sûr.* After some difficulty I was able to track down someone I was told could introduce me to Jean, and I will keep his identity confidential for reasons soon to be obvious. His English wasn't bad, if a bit heavily accented. After offering my condolences on Jean's performance at the 1999 Open, I politely asked him if Jean might be so kind as to help me gain access to play Morfontaine.

Well, he did not directly answer my question. He launched into a tirade against America being a land of over indulgent people living in a crime-ridden, war-mongering society where people are self-centered, eat too much fast food, have an abundance of consumer products, and lack sophistication and culture. I tried to identify the source of his anger, but it appeared deep-seated. At this point, I felt I had nothing to lose and began to suggest an *au contraire*, along the lines that the French seem to elect public figures who are womanizing prima-donnas, are too sensitive, drink too much wine, go on strike too often, and are angry with us because we make better movies than they do, when suddenly the phone disconnected. Perhaps the satellite connection was lost? *Allo . . . Allo . . . Merde.*

Perhaps it was a mistake to start the conversation off bringing up Jean's meltdown at Carnoustie? I was having trouble with the nuances of dealing with the French. I was brought up to believe the United States and France were allies. My feeling was it wouldn't be too difficult for a visiting American to arrange a game at Morfontaine. What surprised me about this episode is the hostility the French have toward Americans. Are we Americans not bosom buddies with the French? Permanent members of the UN Security Council together. We're both members of the nuclear club. Do we not help each other out in times of need? They helped to fund our War of Independence and we helped liberate them in 1944. I do not understand how they're not being more receptive to my inquiries. *Sacré bleu.*

I mustered up the nerve to call the club again to see if they might have softened their previously rigid stance on overseas visitors. Maybe they couldn't hear us clearly last time. I thought it would make sense to speak louder this time and see if that made any difference. It didn't. My latest attempt turned out much the same way the first one did. In fact, probably worse. This time, we thought we heard sounds in the background of a blade being sharpened; could it be they were readying the guillotine at Morfontaine for this obnoxious American? "Jacques, if he calls again, it's off with the head." Rumor has it both the club members and the Fédération Française de Golf were notified about an American *enfant terrible* trying to access their sacred course, and they were warned not to take my calls. Persistence is one of my strong suits, so I mapped out an alternative tactic to try to access Morfontaine.

My exhaustive research led me to the fact that fellow American and golf course architect Kyle Phillips, designer of one of the world's finest courses, Kingsbarns, was hired to make minor changes to the course within the last ten years. Perhaps Mr. Phillips will take my call? Or perhaps the current title holder, the fourteenth Duc de Gramont—whose grandfather founded the course—can help if I appeal to his sense of *noblesse oblige*? Neither option panned out.

Since information about the club was so hard to come by I bought the club's history, which not surprisingly, is written in French. Not to be deterred, I had someone translate it for me. I learned a great deal about the course and its history from the translation, which motivated me to want to play more, although there were discouraging moments based on some of the facts in the book. In golfing lore, the toughest secretary is allegedly at Muirfield in Scotland. Stories of Muirfield secretaries' frosty receptions and methods of turning away visitors are the stuff of legend. Morfontaine apparently can join in the running of having cold-blooded secretaries. Their club history recounts the story of a famous partner in a London law firm who was near the club and went inside to see if he can play. He was rebuffed (I know the feeling) and as he was leaving, saw one of the founders of the club and a member of the British aristocracy. He told the lord how he had always dreamed of playing at Morfontaine and wondered if they could allow him to play as his guest. The lord asked his credentials

Approach to Morfontaine.

and he explained that he is a practicing member of the Church of England; attended Eton; graduated *magna cum laude* from Oxford, where he played four sports; served as a captain in the Coldstream Guards; and fought at Dunkirk, El Alamein, Normandy, and Arnhem, where he won the Distinguished Service Order, Military Cross, and Legion of Honor. Since the distinguished gentleman helped liberate France, they let him play. But only nine holes! See how difficult this can be? If an Oxford-educated war hero can only play nine holes, my chances were slim, but I did not give up. I remained indefatigable in my quest.

Sometimes the best strategy to do is nothing at all for a while and see what happens. I have a friend in San Francisco who is more fanatical than I am. He knew I wanted to play Morfontaine, as did he. He attended a meeting of a local golfing society, and one of the members knew someone in the city, who knew an Englishman, who could connect us to a member of another course in France, who knew a member of Morfontaine. If I did the math right, that makes fives degrees of separation, and it was through these connections I was able to finally play Morfontaine.

In the *Confidential Guide to Golf* Tom Doak classifies Morfontaine as one of the hardest to find locations in the golf world. The drive up from Paris is a tricky one, although the last several kilometers are quaint; you have to drive through a thickly forested area and then down side roads lined with old stone walls. The entrance is easy to miss, set back from the road, partially hidden by trees. Once you manage to find it, the charming drive is befitting this grand club. After you pass through the electronic guard gate, marked *"Propriete Privee. Defense d'Entrer,"* there is a majestic drive lined with mature specimen trees. These type of long entry drives add to the sense of excitement and anticipation when arriving at a first-class club for the first time.

At the end of the winding entry drive in a clearing is their ivy-covered clubhouse, reminiscent of a cozy hunting lodge set in the country. It fits into the landscape like a glove and is unlike any other clubhouse among top golf courses, being quintessentially French. The basement of the clubhouse houses the kitchen. As we approached, I could see down into the kitchen and even at this early hour there were fresh vegetables laid out and being prepared, as well as a half-dozen ducks, which would no doubt later be prepared to perfection.

Morfontaine clubhouse.

As you can see, I research clubs before I play so I can better understand their history and traditions. This is especially important when playing outside the United States since I want to make sure I do not commit any *faux pas*. One of the nice traditions the French have always had is to greet someone with a couple of pecks on the cheek when you meet. First, a kiss to the left cheek, then a kiss to the right cheek. I wanted to respect this custom and display the proper protocol at Morfontaine, so upon entry into the clubhouse I tried to do the old double-kiss routine with the secretary, but was rebuffed. Either my halitosis put him off, or I came in at the wrong angle, but I felt this well-coiffed gentleman thought there was something wrong with me.

As we sat in the clubhouse, a female employee arrived with a large bag of fresh baguettes. It couldn't have been more alluring, our expectations of a full-blooded French golf experience were exceeded at every turn. To give you a sense of the classy nature of Morfontaine, above the fireplace in the clubhouse is a putter made out of gold given to the club by Louis Cartier, the famous watchmaker. The ambiance of the clubhouse is warm and inviting, and it is not hard to imagine you are back in the 1920s and a Grand Duc yourself. The misty morning I was there added to the romance of Morfontaine. I honestly could have sat in the clubhouse for hours drinking coffee and hanging out. The staff made us some fresh coffee, which in retrospect was a mistake, since coffee in France is more akin to double espresso, and I did not need to be more pumped up. My heart was racing fast by the time we set off to play golf.

Although this book does not delve into the history of golf clubs, I am making an exception with regard to Morfontaine because they have a fascinating one which I learned when I had the club history translated. As I said, there are twenty-seven holes of golf at Morfontaine: the 9-hole Valliere course, built in 1911, and the 18-hole championship course, built in 1927. The course was overrun in June 1940 by the Third Reich when they captured Paris. The Germans drove Panzer tanks on the course and caused deep ruts in many fairways and greens, particularly on the 9th and 10th holes; the 8th hole was hit by artillery shells and they set up a cannon on the 13th green that did serious damage. Many of the greenkeeping staff and club members joined the army or were taken prisoner during this time, putting serious stress on the club's survival.

The Nazis ransacked the clubhouse and looted food and items of value during the occupation. After the German troops left, Commandant Soldatenkoff, the club secretary, took charge to restore the course to some semblance of normalcy. Soldatenkoff was a retired commandant from the Imperial Russian Marines and the club history describes him as elegant and funny. By December 1940 he had the course restored to a basic level of functioning. During the war, gasoline was at a premium, so they had to use horses to operate the equipment to re-grade the damaged holes and cut the grass. They put leather boots on the horses so their hoofs did not further damage the course. Commandant Soldatenkoff organized a bus from Paris each Sunday during the war for members that wanted to play. There was no food service or other amenities, so members brought their own food and drink. During this time, parts of the Valliere course were used to grow potatoes to help members and locals survive.

In November 1942 a four-engine RAF bomber was shot down by the Germans as it was returning from a bomb run on Stuttgart. The plane crash-landed in the polo grounds next to the course and four members of the crew, including the pilot, were taken back to the clubhouse to be cared for. The winter of 1943 was so harsh that trees on the course had to be cut down to be used as firewood to keep warm. After a full recovery in the postwar period, the course was played by the rich and famous includ-

The par-3 4th hole, Morfontaine Valliere course.

ing Gary Cooper, Bing Crosby, Jerry Lewis, Bob Hope, the king of Spain, the king of Belgium, and the duke of Windsor. General Eisenhower was an honorary member during the years he served as NATO commander and played the course a half-dozen times after the war and was fond of it. He primarily played with other senior military officers but also played there with Conrad N. Hilton. Among other correspondence at Eisenhower's Presidential Library is a letter from the founding Duc de Gramont letting Ike know he was thrilled to have him playing there.

The course is built in a forest and has an abundance of heather, reminiscent of the heathland courses outside of London, such as Walton Heath. The soil is naturally sandy and thus ideally suited for good golf, and there are ferns growing vigorously all over the property. It is a good walking course since almost all the tee boxes are near the previous greens. Simpson designed large greens at Morfontaine and left many of the natural rock outcroppings in place, which adds to the character of the course. Simpson is my kind of fellow; he had a flair for the dramatic. He once drove his Rolls-Royce slowly up and down in front of a club committee's window as they deliberated whether to accept his design as an architect. He was on record as saying that no golf hole could be truly great unless it began to occupy the player's mind before they came to it, and said, "The vital thing about a hole is that it should either be more difficult than it looks or look more difficult than it is. It must never be what it looks." He designed his courses to demand "mental agility." Seeing Morfontaine makes it clear to me that the man had talents far beyond ordinary golf course architects. Morfontaine is an absolute treasure and work of art; it has that certain something the French call *je ne sais quoi* that sets it apart from anywhere else I have ever played golf. Similar to Yeamans Hall, which is set on a 900-acre former plantation site in Charleston, the entire atmosphere and sense of isolation at Morfontaine envelops you.

One of the biggest surprises of all my travels was the 9-hole Valliere course. I thought the Valliere had more character than the 18-hole course, which is saying something. The Valliere is a cross between Cruden Bay (idiosyncratic) and Walton Heath (heathlands), a delightfully quirky and very fun round of golf. The captivating 3rd hole is one of the best I have ever played. It plays from an elevated tee engulfed in heather, down into a valley filled with rock outcroppings. The fairway slopes right to left the length of the hole. The 4th hole at Valliere is a world-class par-3 that plays downhill and is surrounded by bunkers almost the entire way around. There is also a sea of heather in front of the hole and tons of ferns to the right side and behind it. It has a false front to the green, creating an optical illusion from the tee.

We used the Valliere course as a warmup in the morning before playing the championship course, had a nice lunch in the clubhouse, and were so impressed with the Valliere that we played it again after lunch for a happy thirty-six holes of golf. The wine was as spectacular as the food, which was superbly prepared, as anticipated. In keeping with the French aversion to commercialism, the "pro shop" at Morfontaine is a closet with some shirts, sweaters, and hats. You know when the "pro shop" is open when they open the door and put the light on in the closet. One of the treasured possessions of my golf travels is a lime-green golf shirt with their club logo on it that I was able to convince the secretary to sell to me.

The reality is I have always had a great affection for France: the food, the wine, the sound of the language, the culture, and the sense of style and ceremony that surrounds every aspect of French life. I am also a fan of French cinema, Paris's old cobblestone streets, the beauty of the countryside, the distinctive police sirens, formal French gardens, and *tous les chiche femmes*. The more I think about it, it is difficult to dislike a culture that has a device in the bathroom that washes your buttocks and where you are guaranteed five weeks' vacation.

Despite my early difficulties trying to access this private French course—or perhaps more so because of them—this was one of the best experiences of my journey. Morfontaine can't be fairly compared to any other club I've ever been to. It is private, intimate, and beguiling. The club has advanced somewhat over the years—they now have a website and an email address, although they are in French only. While this is clearly progress, to save you the effort of translating the website or emailing them, their simple answer to all is still *non. Bon chance* as you try to play Morfontaine.

Chantilly, another Tom Simpson course outside of Paris, near Morfontaine, is also worth playing. It too has a cozy clubhouse and an outstanding lunch. In England or the United States you often see people having a couple of beers after a round, in Scotland you can catch locals occasionally taking a wee nip from their flask during the round, and in a classic French move, here, it's a bottle of Bordeaux or Burgundy after the round. Chantilly is more wide-open than Morfontaine and doesn't have as much heather, but it has been used as a venue for the French Open, and if you can get an invitation it's well worth going. Chantilly's website is more helpful than Morfontaine's, but a bit rough on their English translations. Among other details listed in their dress code are "no long-line bra nor straps for women." Perhaps short-line bras or strapless bras are permitted?

Vive la France!

Loch Lomond

Having tackled continental Europe, I now shift back across the English Channel. Which golf course is the toughest to access in the British Isles? Well, in my case it was Loch Lomond, located thirty miles north of Glasgow. I had completed playing twenty-three of the twenty-four courses I was trying to play in the British Isles, and Loch Lomond proved the most difficult, and the only one I still needed to play. As I have outlined, although most private clubs in the British Isles follow long-standing tradition and allow visitors to book a round as long as you follow their rules and protocols, Loch Lomond does not. It is a very private affair. You must play with a member, so I could not call the club and book a round.

Loch Lomond has one of the most unusual approaches I have ever seen to membership. Organized in 1994, Loch Lomond was setup in the tradition of Augusta and Pine Valley. It has an international membership, and, for the most part, doesn't serve as a local golf club in the traditional sense. In fact, according to the club, it was constituted as a "destination" club to be "savored" only a few times a year. Loch Lomond has accommodations where members can stay overnight in either the mansion or in lodges bordering the glens along the shore of the loch. When it was established membership was organized around specific geographic regions; the club appointed specific "Club Captains" to assume leadership and membership responsibilities for those geographic regions, and to ensure a particular geographic mix of members. They claim to have members from over forty countries. The brainchild of the club was Lyle Anderson, a real estate developer from Phoenix and an Augusta member.

I was flipping through a brochure they put together about the club and they describe themselves as a "private and discerning international golf club." Their P.R. sounded a bit pious to me. They described Loch Lomond as "a singular place to meet on the world stage . . . It is a sanctuary not just for golf aficionados but for world thinkers." What does that mean? World thinkers? So it's the Davos of golf clubs? The United Nations of the links? Their marketing piece was like something written by a chain-smoking, over-lipsticked, highly-caffeinated realtor in Nevada: adjectives gone

Loch Lomond's clubhouse, Rossdhu House.

wild. I came away with the feeling that they raised their pinkies when having cocktails at Loch Lomond. Also taken from their marketing literature, "Loch Lomond has a state-of-the-art, exceptionally amenitized spa in a walled garden." An exceptionally amenitized spa? What is an amenitized spa?

At the time, members of this high-minded club included Sir Sean Connery, Sir Nick Faldo, Ernie Els, Colin Montgomerie, and His Royal Highness Prince Andrew. The club has an unusual feature I have never heard of before; they limit the amount of play *members* may have. Most clubs have a limit on guest play, but I've never heard of limiting member play; members are limited to playing the course no more than fourteen times in any given year; their guest policy is therefore, by definition, restrictive.

Although the club is exclusive, the course is known to the public because the week before the Open Championship the Scottish Open used to be played here. This allowed outsiders a peek at what has been called the most beautiful setting in the world, although I'm sure Donald Trump would take exception to this characterization, because all his courses have a monopoly on descriptions using such phrases. The property is 680 acres in total and their clubhouse, Rossdhu House, serves as a focal point in the scenery, with the loch and the mountains in the background.

Their approach to running the golf club did not work out as planned. They entered into receivership in late 2008 during the financial crisis, around the time I was trying to play it, which made it more difficult for me. I had talked to two members over the years but both dropped out due to the increasingly high dues and the restrictions. I was offered a chance to play, but they were so desperate for revenue the guest greens fee was £600 ($900), so I passed, because it's wrong. At best, a guest at most top courses is $250, often less.

As part of the club's reorganization, Scotland's *The Herald* newspaper reported their 850 members, "who already pay a joining fee of £55,000 ($82,500) and an annual subscription of around £4,000 ($6,000), will be asked to contribute financially to secure the sale of the prestigious club, which is home of the Scottish Open." The club survived the crisis and is now member-owned as I understand it.

I was invited to the club a year later after being introduced to a member, and it proved to be magnificent. Perhaps, there was something behind all that hype. Loch

Lomond is one of the finest and most scenic places in the world to be at and to play golf. What makes it so charming is the combination of having an outstanding course set in a breathtaking location, plus the exclusivity of the club, and one of the best clubhouses in the world. The golf course, designed by Tom Weiskopf and Jay Morrish, matches the beauty of the setting. Although the course is criticized by some, unjustly in my view, because it is not a links layout, it is impossible to separate the course from its environment. Looked at in total, I would say Loch Lomond is one of the top twenty-five places in the world to play golf; no matter what direction you look while at Loch Lomond it is awe-inspiring.

If someone knows of a finer clubhouse in the entire world than Rossdhu House, please let me know. The clubhouses at the National Golf Links, Winged Foot, Seminole, Congressional, Garden City, Shinnecock Hills, and the Honourable Company of Edinburgh Golfers impressed me as being world-class. Rossdhu House takes it to another level. The similarities between Loch Lomond and the White House are striking. The club has an exterior fence around the property with a gate-guarded entrance. Your movements on the property are orchestrated with precision; when you arrive and leave employees of the club track your progress with walkie-talkies through a command center. The interior of their Georgian mansion has a series of interconnected themed rooms, each decorated with original, high-quality, large oil paintings. Rossdhu House has a green room, a red room, a library, a formal dining room, a reception area, and a series of additional rooms for a variety of specialized purposes I lost count of. Further paralleling 1600 Pennsylvania Avenue, the club has its own helicopter. Each has a Rose Garden and elaborately manicured grounds. Rossdhu House even one-ups the White House with clearly superior views out of their large windows, and I doubt the White House has an amenitized spa.

In the end, I was won over at Loch Lomond by the setting and the Scottish charm. There was a mail boat going up and down the loch delivering mail the day I played, adding to the timelessness of the setting. Despite their over-the-top marketing brochure, the club is not pretentious; the member that hosted me is one of the finest people I have ever met, and I've decided I like being pampered. I had an "A" caddie and an invigorating day at Loch Lomond.

The approach to Loch Lomond's 10th hole.

It was at Loch Lomond I officially became a golf snob. I grew up without playing golf; I took it up later in life, and one of the big mistakes I made was not taking lessons early on, so I have been trying to learn the proper way to play for the last thirty years. I know it sounds shocking given the courses I have written about, but the majority of the golf I have played in my life has been on public courses, where people often do not replace divots, ball marks are not always repaired, and normally there is a wait on every hole for the group ahead to hit their shots. I was not called Mr. Sabino or "sir." Nobody shined my street shoes while I was out playing the course, and nobody cleaned my golf shoes after the round, standard fare at all these clubs. The problem is, once you experience this level of golf, it is tough to go back. Experiences such as Loch Lomond spoil you; everything fits together perfectly, you play on a manicured course at a quick pace without waiting, with caddies carrying your bag. I apologize to all you hackers out there for leaving the fraternity of regular guys and moving over to the dark side. I have gone native. It did strike me as a bit odd that they served us Kool-Aid after the round, in the walled garden they mentioned in their marketing brochure. I should have paid more attention because it didn't seem right at the time, but now there is no going back.

In keeping with the high-end nature of the club, Loch Lomond prints custom scorecards each day, adjusting the yardages for where the tees are set and illustrating the *actual* pin placements. On the day we played the cards were not accurate, which is frankly no big deal. It is easy enough to look at the green and figure out where the pin is. After the 3rd hole, the caddies knew something was wrong. In classic Scottish fashion we heard from the various caddies in succession, "The scorecards are rubbish today," "These sheets are all shite," in a way only a Scotsman can pull it off. It is one of the endearing charms of Scotland that without intending to do so, almost everything the Scots say, to the American ear, is tinged with deadpan humor and sarcasm. The Scots use their words sparingly, but always with maximum impact. Loch Lomond was worth the wait and a fitting way to close out my Scottish golfing education.

CHAPTER NINE
Golfing in Zululand, South Africa

Many of the world's great golf courses are clustered together and traveling to one course affords you the opportunity to play others nearby. The Bandon Resort is a prime example, as is the Sandbelt region of Melbourne and the Monterey Peninsula. Sometimes, a course sits all alone in isolation, in the case of the course we are about to look at, alone on its own continent.

Beyond compulsiveness and impatience, the third aspect that rounds out my delightful personality is impulsiveness. One long winter holiday I told my wife I was going out to play golf and she gave me one of those looks, since it was blustery and damp outside and she knew I was up to something. It just popped into my head as one of those spur-of-the-moment deals; I could leave for a few days and play a course I had always wanted to. This quest has been a journey of self-discovery, and I discovered that a solo golf trip to the Southern Hemisphere works wonders for my mood. Almost all my trips have been with friends, but sometimes I find it cathartic to simply do a golf trip all by myself. It is the antidote to being stuck in the house with cabin fever, especially because I do not ski.

I thought traveling to Royal Dornoch in the Scottish Highlands, and to Sand Hills in Nebraska was difficult; Durban Country Club was significantly more so. Durban is located in the South African province of KwaZulu-Natal. This area, now called the Zulu Kingdom, formerly known as the Zululand, took me more than twenty-four hours to travel to once I left my house. I flew back-to-back red-eyes with a change of planes in London, and a final, a two-hour flight to Durban on South African Airways. Durban is not only Africa's largest and busiest port city, but also a beach resort that reminded me of a cross between Miami and Mumbai; picture it as 1960s South Beach, but with saris instead of bikinis. A subtropical city, Durban grew rapidly in the late nineteenth and early twentieth centuries when its main industry, sugarcane, was booming. Many laborers from India were sent to South Africa during this period as indentured servants. Remnants of this historical period remain within the fabric of Durban today; the city still has a large Indian population, the largest concentration outside of India, and it remains a major working port and center for sugar. Driving in from the airport to the city center, the roads are lined with warehouses, sugar processing plants, and grain elevators. I found a sharp contrast between Durban and the more polished and cosmopolitan Cape Town.

Durban Country Club is private, but they allow visitors if you call or email them and reserve a time. I was able to secure some tee times over a two-day period, on short notice.

Durban has several notable aspects among the top 100 courses. It is the only one located on the Indian Ocean, the only one on the continent of Africa, and the course located closest to the Tropic of Capricorn. The course is located ten minutes from the city center between a rugby stadium and the Indian Ocean. An eclectic design, Durban was shaped from the bush and dunes during the early 1920s by two local golf professionals: George Waterman and Laurie Waters. Colonel S. V. Hotchkin—who worked extensively on one of my favorite English courses, Woodhall Spa—made changes to Durban in 1928, and finally additional changes were made by South African architect Bob Grimsdell in 1959.

The course is not directly on the ocean, it is separated from it by a busy highway, and the imposing Moses Mabhida Stadium towers over the last couple of holes on the back nine. I liked Durban because it has some characteristics not commonly seen on other courses, most notably its routing through "the bush." It has a particularly strong start, especially the first five holes, which are narrow and hilly and play in the bush. The middle holes—excluding No. 12—are not remarkable, but the course finishes

Durban's 2nd hole plays through "the bush."

strong, especially the last three holes. The front nine are near the Indian Ocean, and are therefore more impacted by the wind. On the first day I played, there were many windsurfers and parasailers out on the white-capped sea enjoying the strong wind, which usually isn't a good sign for golf, but it turned out not to be too bad because the course is sheltered.

At Durban, there is not trouble in the traditional sense we find it in the United States or British Isles with high grass or rough off the fairways. Instead, off many of the fairways is thick sub-tropical vegetation, and the bush is largely unplayable if your ball goes in it. In vestiges of its British colonial heritage, local rules at Durban indicate what to do should balls inadvertently come to rest on one of the two grass bowling greens on the property.

The par-5 3rd hole is one of the best in the world I have had the privilege to play. It has a high elevated tee with a view of the Indian Ocean, and it requires you to hit down into a narrow valley, surrounded on both sides by thick bush. When down in the fairway you can't hear any external noise, including the ocean or the highway. What you can hear is the wildlife and birds chirping. I saw several exotic birds, including the brilliant scarlet-chested sunbird flying back and forth between the trees on this hole. The wildlife is so plentiful the club allows visiting bird watchers to tour the course. Once through playing the hole, you walk off the elevated green and along a narrow path carved in the bush to climb to the next tee box. This same scene is repeated on the next hole's green-to-tee walk as well.

There is a halfway house with seating between the 9th and 10th holes. The custom at Durban is to stop and have some beverages and food, which every group did both

My gallery on the 16th hole at Durban.

days I was there. Since you are in the tropics, the need to cool down and take a break from the heat and humidity trumps the need to keep playing and complete a round quickly.

I find golf to be such a rejuvenating pursuit because it allows you to commune with nature. While playing the 16th hole I had a true Durban-esque experience, and was very close to nature. I hit my tee shot into the left rough on this par-4, near the bush and under a tree. As I walked over to assess my lie, a monkey dropped from the tree to look the ball and me over. The look on his face told me he wasn't particularly impressed with my tee shot. He sat nearby and watched me hit my second shot fat, or

Durban Country Club, 17th fairway.

as my caddie summed up in the local parlance with his thick Afrikaans accent, "it was a rank shot." In my defense, it is hard to concentrate with a monkey as your gallery. I ended up making a double bogey, or, as it is called in South Africa, a "double drop."

So how is it a course with nine average holes wedged between two concrete structures is ranked in the world's top 100? Similar to Pebble Beach, because the good holes are so good, they more than compensate for the weak holes. Plus, the attraction of playing in the bush makes it unique. The fairways were built on wavy sand dunes and have a rough-hewn look; one of the defining characteristics at Durban is the untamed undulations in the fairways, and it is a testament to each of the designers that had a hand in shaping the course that they all had the foresight to leave well enough alone, and didn't smooth out all the ripples.

My caddie the first day at Durban didn't wear shoes, as many of them here do not; instead they carry bags around barefooted. There was no motorized ball machine on the narrow driving range; instead caddies pick up and clean each ball as you hit them. Durban is an inspiring golf course and was in exceptionally good condition when I played there, especially the unusual "umgeni" grass greens.

Sewsunker "Papwa" Sewgolum

I was joined by a member of Indian descent on the second day I played, and he was gracious and accommodating. We sat in the clubhouse afterward admiring the spectacular view over a couple of drinks, and he mentioned the story of "Papwa" to me.

One of the unexpected benefits of this quest is discovering some of the lesser-known stories in the history of golf, such as those of Jim Wysocki and Ralph Kennedy. Another lesser-known but compelling story is of Sewsunker Sewgolum, whose nickname was Papwa. In 1963, Sewsunker, a five-foot-four-inch, 150-pound caddie and self-taught golfer of Indian descent became the first non-white to compete in a white-only tournament in South Africa, the Natal Open, played at Durban. He had the temerity to win the tournament, beating a field of 113 white golfers. During the awards ceremony, Sewsunker was presented the trophy in the pouring rain while the white club membership were snug inside the clubhouse, watching in dry splendor. The white runners-up were also awarded their prizes in the clubhouse. Sewsunker played and won under crushing adversity; he took his meals during the tournament with the black caddies and had to change his clothes in a car. The South African Broadcasting Corporation, which was government-owned at the time, canceled coverage of the tournament once Papwa entered, and did not report the results on its news program. All this occurred at the height of the apartheid period in South Africa. When the picture showing Sewsunker receiving the trophy in the rain was shown around the world it caused an outrage and put pressure on the government to change its apartheid policies.

The club's 1982 history includes a comical explanation of why he was slighted: "The laws of the day were such that Indian people were not allowed inside the clubhouse. An infraction of those laws could have resulted in the club losing its liquor license and being closed down." They state if they had moved the ceremony inside, Sewsunker's fans wouldn't have been able to see him receive the trophy. To quote, "It certainly was not a slight to Papwa—rather one of consideration to enable his fans to see him in his moment of victory."

In 1965, in the same tournament, Sewsunker played again and finished first, beating a field that included Gary Player, who won the US Open that same year. Unfortunately his success was short-lived; the following year he was banned from all local tournaments and the Apartheid government withdrew his passport, preventing him from playing internationally. He could not even enter courses as a spectator. Prior to the ban, Sewsunker played in the South African PGA tournament while two government agents followed him around the course to make sure segregation laws were enforced. Under the laws at the time, non-whites could play only among themselves before spectators who were non-white, and the crowds at the tournament were segregated. During this period, security police regularly followed him around and harassed and threatened him frequently. He had to apply for permits to play in white tournaments, and sometimes they were granted but often times they were not. In another offensive remark in the club history, they wrote, "Sadly, brilliant golfer that he was, Papwa seemed to lack the determination and discipline to remain at the top."

Prior to the ban, Sewsunker successfully competed internationally. While he was not caddying, Sewgolum worked in an Oil of Olay factory putting the tops onto filled bottles. He was befriended by the founder and owner of Oil of Olay, who took him to Europe to play. Prior to going on his first trip in 1959, however, they had to teach him how to write his name so that he could sign his scorecards, since he was illiterate. He had to learn how to use a knife and fork, since previously he had only eaten with his hands. Before he was banned, Sewgolum won the Dutch Open Championships in 1959, 1960, and 1964. He played in the Open Championship a handful of times, including at Muirfield in 1959 and at Royal Lytham in 1963, where he made the cut; he shot 71 in the first round, the same as Jack Nicklaus, and through thirty-six holes he was tied with Gary Player and two strokes ahead of Arnold Palmer.

What makes Sewsunker's story even more amazing is he played the game with a back-handed grip, hands positioned the opposite way to the traditional grip. The unorthodox grip is now known as the Sewsunker grip, named after Sewgolum because he used it with such success. Imagine for a minute a kack-handed grip, as it is sometimes called. The game is hard enough; could you imagine as a right-handed golfer holding the club with your left hand beneath your right? Pick up a club and try swinging it that way and you will feel how hard it is.

"Papwa" Sewsunker (Ranjith Kally).

Unfortunately, golf has had a history of excluding people of color, and while not a proud chapter at many of the top country clubs, it is a chapter nonetheless. Papwa's story reminded me that what Lee Elder, Charlie Sifford, Tiger Woods, and others have been able to accomplish is all the more admirable given the history of segregation and apartheid. South African president Thabo Mbeki bestowed a posthumous achievement award on Papwa in 2003, and to their credit, Durban honored him as well, creating a memorial plaque, unveiled in 2005, a year before I visited. Club chairman Ray Lalouette described the 1963 Natal Open awards ceremony as, "an ignominious debacle that must have been the source of much embarrassment and humiliation for a fellow human being at a time when he should have been experiencing joy and jubilation."

I played Durban at roughly the midpoint of my 100-course quest, and it was a memorable way to celebrate the half way point of my goal. I am a believer in fate, and in what I took as a good omen, I bumped into the Nobel Peace Prize winner Archbishop Desmond Tutu coming out of the lavatory on my flight back from Cape Town to London. Although my hair was sticking straight up after ten hours in a coach seat, he gave me a big smile and a friendly hello. As it turned out, meeting His Grace was a positive sign, because the best was yet to come.

So, if you're ever bored at home during a drizzly and gray winter in the Northern Hemisphere, remember, a trip to the warmth of South Africa could be just what you need to lift you out of your funk.

CHAPTER TEN
Golf in Japan

I am fortunate to have taken more than my fair share of golf trips. My traveling companions and I are simpatico, which is rare, since it is hard to find a group that meshes well together. Traveling with people is demanding, because everyone has their little peculiarities and nuances and generally people want to do different things, eat at different places, or are selfish. My fellow itinerant golfers are agreeable (except for their deafening snoring) and have good senses of humor. When people ask me what my greatest trip of all was, I usually answer it was Japan, partly because of my companions. I have done some unbelievable golf trips to New Zealand, Australia, Ireland, and Scotland; as my wife consistently reminded me every time I was asking permission to book one, I always said they were "once-in-a-lifetime" trips. My trip to Japan was on a different plane than all the others. The uniqueness of the culture, combined with the golf rituals Japan has developed, make it a special place to play.

Japan is one of the more homogeneous societies in the world and is geared toward the Japanese. In discussions with other people who have played the top 100 I always ask how they played the Japanese courses, because I know they are hard to access. Almost all of them did so through business contacts; that is, they knew an executive at a Japanese company or did business with a company with strong contacts in Japan. If you can pursue this route, it is your best bet. I was not able to, and there are almost no good methods to gain access to private courses in Japan. Finding a member of a private course on your own, given the language barrier, is difficult. Many of the other techniques I have outlined in earlier chapters similarly won't work; they do not have charity outings you can play in and your club pro almost certainly can't help.

The most effective way to access the private courses in Japan is to go on a bespoke golf tour with a high-end operator. A company such as GolfTI in Canada has done trips to Japan in the past and has accessed courses most people want to play, including the Tokyo Golf Club, the Hirono Golf Club, and the Naruo Golf Club. I accessed the courses in Japan through a company named Japan Golf Tours that no longer exists. It was run by a Japanese-speaking American golf pro who grew up in North Carolina. He knew members at the best clubs and would arrange tours for obsessed Americans, yours truly included. While it is not an inexpensive way to pursue the clubs, there are not many other options.

From my point of view, having someone who speaks the language is imperative, as is having a driver who can navigate the tricky routes to the courses, some of which—especially Kawana—are in remote locations with no English translations on the road signs. While in Japan we traveled using cars arranged by the tour company, and we took the *Shinkansen* bullet train, which was a treat.

The Golf Courses

The good news to start off with is the Fuji Course at the Kawana Golf Hotel, one of the best courses in the world, is a resort, and you can play there by booking in advance and staying at the on-property hotel. Often called Japan's Pebble Beach because it is a resort set on cliffs near the ocean, Kawana is located in Shizuoka Prefecture, two hours from Tokyo on the Izu Peninsula, in a national park on Sagami Bay. The course was completed in 1936 by Charles H. Alison, one-time partner of H. S. Colt. Alison took a vacation at the Kawana Hotel in 1930 and convinced the owner he should use the amazing land to build a golf course. During the Second World War almost all the golf courses in Japan had to be converted into farmland to produce food—in fact only seventeen courses survived the war. After the war Hotel Kawana was taken over by the U.S. Eighth Army and was later handed over to the Australian troops to be converted into a recreation center. Kawana has the feel of the Bay Area in San Francisco and many

Kawana Fuji Course, Japan, par-5 15th hole.

of the interior holes reminded me of the Olympic Club, with narrow, tree-lined, and sloping fairways. Kawana is impressive and the par-5 15th hole, which runs along the edge of a rocky cliff, is as breathtaking as anything you'll see at Pebble Beach. The hole plays from an elevated tee down into a valley, then gently rises up to the crest of a hill until it reaches the green; the entire hole plays along an elevated headland, with the waves of the Pacific crashing dramatically below.

Hirono Golf Club is Japan's most distinguished, located near the port city of Kobe. We took the bullet train down from Tokyo to Kobe, and the course is less than an hour's drive from there. Hirono is a private course and you must play with a member.

The course was built by Alison in 1932, on an estate that was previously owned by a feudal warlord, and it is his masterpiece and the highest-ranked course in Japan. The course has some similarities to Pine Valley, with an imaginative routing and varied holes. As with Pine Valley, most holes are isolated from the others by dense trees, and you can't see adjoining holes while playing your hole. The par-3s at Hirono are especially strong and the course is one of the best conditioned I have ever seen. The greens and fairways are in meticulous condition and even the trees throughout the course are manicured from top to bottom, in the manner of a Japanese garden. It has all the key elements present in Alison's Japanese courses: strategic bunkering, small elevated

Hirono, Japan, 13th hole in manicured grounds.

greens, double doglegs, and forced carries over ravines. Hirono is a hilly course, so hilly that in one part of the course they have installed an outdoor escalator to carry you up the hill.

Naruo Golf Club is located in the mountains between Kobe and Osaka and is also a private course where you must play with a member. The course was designed by Scottish professionals Joe Crane and H. C. Crane in 1904, with revisions made by Alison in 1930. The course was founded by British expatriates and is Japan's hidden gem. Naruo is narrow, quirky, and difficult. The greens at Naruo are "korai," which is a thick grass similar to Bermuda, and they are slow, running about an eight on the stimpmeter. We stayed at a traditional Japanese *ryokan* when we played Naruo, with tatami-matted rooms as well as communal baths; our meals were prepared for us in our rooms, followed by a pre-bedtime massage. It is a very civilized country.

If you ever have the opportunity to play Naruo, I suggest doing some training beforehand because you need to be fit. The course is built on terrain that is steep, and it is one of the most difficult courses I have ever walked. How difficult? So much so that they have a built-in traction system around all eighteen holes to relieve the caddies from having to push the carts up and down the rugged terrain. The mechanized system works with magnets under the ground and the caddie controls it by remote control. The property at Naruo reminded me of Bel-Air because it is a relatively small piece of landlocked, hilly property, and at Bel-Air during your round you take an elevator because of the steep terrain. The Japanese have an attention to detail that defines their society, and it is the small touches that sometimes leave the most lasting impressions. At the 15th tee there is a traditional Japanese-style wooden house where you take a break and have a cup of tea before playing the hole.

I also played the Tokyo Golf Club while in Japan, which has a long and complicated history. It originally opened in 1914 on leased land, then moved to a new location in a design done by Alison in 1932. Unfortunately, the land and course were seized by the Imperial Japanese Army during World War II. The current course, and the third incarnation, was built by Kohmyo Ohtani in 1940 based on the earlier layout by Alison. It is located in Sayama City, about an hour and a half outside the city center. The U.S. Army took over the course in 1946 and returned it to the members in 1952.

Naruo, Japan, 10th hole.

Tokyo Golf Club was the hardest of all the private courses in Japan to get on. It's the equivalent of Muirfield in terms of its exclusivity and traditions, although the guest greens fee was reasonable, at about $200. Our tour operator wasn't able to arrange for us to play; instead, I was invited by a Japanese reader of my blog who had emailed me the year before and offered to host us.

Tokyo is distinctive relative to any other course I have played because it has multiple holes with two sets of greens. Because it is so hot and humid in the summer in Japan, the greens are planted with different types of grass. One set of greens has grass that does well in cool weather and the other has a strain that thrives in warm weather.

Another of Alison's Japanese-designed courses is immediately next door to Tokyo Golf Club and runs parallel to holes No. 11 and 12: Kasumigaseki, whose East course is well-regarded. Originally designed by an amateur golfer and businessman, Alison modified the course, and it is well-known for its deep bunkers, which the Japanese have nicknamed with an odd pronunciation of his name, "Arisons." Kasumigaseki will host the Olympic golf events when the games return to Tokyo in 2020.

Japanese Golf Traditions and Etiquette

Japan is a highly ritualized and organized society and playing golf in Japan is no exception to their ordered lives. Playing in Japan can be more accurately described as a "day of golf" rather than a "round of golf." This is not a country where you throw your bag over your shoulder and walk nine holes after work. I offer the following dozen pieces of advice to my fellow golf adventurers traveling to the Land of the Rising Sun:

1. Learn some basic Japanese. The word *arigato* means thank you, and if you say it about 300 times a round, you're off to a good start. It is also acceptable to say, "goo shot" if a Japanese player hits a good shot. I know it sounds goofy, but it's a bastardized English expression you hear often. The word "-san" after a name is a sign of respect, so if your host's name is "Oizumi," you refer to him as "Oizumi-san."

2. Wear a jacket when arriving at a private club; in the manner of Garden City and Muirfield, the proper protocol when arriving at a private Japanese club is to wear a jacket.

3. Arrive on time. Do not arrive early and do not arrive late. In a country where subway trains arrive the second they are supposed to, there is a premium put on punctuality. Bow when you meet your host and thank him profusely for hosting you. Bring a small gift and give it to him when you meet; I gave golf books to my hosts and they were most grateful.

4. Check-in for your round. When you arrive at the club there is a reception area similar to a hotel check-in and you receive a little card holder and locker key. If you want to buy something in the pro shop or halfway-house, you sign chits with your

assigned number and everything is charged to the card; as you leave, you settle the bill. Credit cards are accepted, but oddly enough, as with most transactions in Japan, they prefer cash.

5. Have a pre-round cup of coffee, if offered. All three hosts offered me coffee before the round, which you take sitting in the grill room as a prelude to the round.

6. There is no tipping at golf clubs in Japan, period. This includes caddies, locker room attendants, et cetera.

7. Sign the sheet the caddie hands you. When you arrive at the first tee your caddie will have your bag already loaded on a cart and will have counted your clubs. You are asked to sign off on the number of clubs in your bag before teeing off and at the conclusion of the round. Since she won't speak English and the sheet she hands you is

Japanese caddie.

in *kanji*, it took me a while to understand what it was. At first I took the sheet, hit her with a barrage of *"arigatos,"* with a couple of slight bows, and nodded continuously—although my first caddy was persistent and wouldn't stop handing me the form until I signed it. It all made sense after it was explained to me. Caddies in Japan are almost all women and they dress in the most unusual manner possible. All the ones we had wore helmet-style hats draped with long white handkerchiefs over them, long pants, two gloves, long-sleeved shirts, and white rubber boots; they are covered head-to-toe so they avoid exposure to the sun. Visualize Darth Vader in a light-green prison outfit, with a white hat.

8. There are no "gimme" putts. I'm not sure if this is true all over Japan, but the members I played with at all three private courses followed strict stroke-play rules and didn't give any putts, not even a three-inch tap in.

9. Play with long pants and bring your rain gear. Summers in Japan are hot and humid and it would be nice to wear shorts, but long pants are required at private clubs. Their rainy season is June through October, so it is best to go in the spring if you can.

10. Stop for lunch after nine holes. Unlike in the United Kingdom and United States where you play eighteen holes straight through, in Japan you stop after nine holes and have lunch. The appropriate protocol at lunch is to have beer before your meal and coffee afterward. I suggest having both wherever you go because it is easy to insult your host if you do not take everything that is offered. When I played Hirono I didn't feel like having a beer and received the appropriate subtle scolding from our host—one of many screwups Sabino-san made while there. If you are not an adventurous eater and are worried about being served fish heads, most clubs serve a curried beef dish with rice you can fall back on.

Some courses will give you a back nine starting time as you go in for lunch, others allow you to tee off when you are ready. I stiffened up at lunch because we typically sat there for a good ninety minutes, making the 10th a hole that is hard to play well; hitting a good drive with a stiff back and a light head is not one of my strengths. Another Japanese tradition is that you do not pour your own beer. When your glass is half empty someone else at the table picks up the bottle and pours more into your glass; so keep your eye out for someone whose glass needs filling, and be patient for someone to pour more into your glass.

11. Take the post-round communal hot bath. After the round, the fun really begins. The high point of any Japanese golfing experience is the bath, known as *o-furo*. In your assigned locker you are given a pair of small plastic slippers—mine were about three sizes too small for my feet. After you finish playing you take off your golf shoes and put on the slippers; leave your clothes on, but take a change of clothes with you and head toward the bath area. As you enter, take off your slippers and walk to a changing area filled with baskets. Only here do you take off your clothes and grab a small towel.

As I learned the hard way, whatever you do at this point do not grab a large towel, it is a breach of protocol and I sent members near me into a flailing frenzy when I did so. You then enter the shower area with your hand towel; there are western-style showers available which are acceptable to use, but most Japanese men sit on foot-high little wooden stools and wash themselves vigorously out in a big open area with a handheld showerhead. Japanese men are reserved in all aspects of their lives except washing themselves in public. They embrace the task with such élan that I was taken aback each time I saw it. After you have finished cleaning up, the custom is to take a communal hot bath. We're talking buck naked, boys; no towels to hide behind and no bathing suits allowed. Picture fifteen of your geriatric best friends together in a large hot tub, immersed in water up to their necks, and you get the idea. Some of the bathers put the little towel on top of their heads during the bath, which makes them look like some sort of escapee from a lunatic asylum. The whole scene comes straight out of a Fellini movie.

The biggest *faux pas* possible would be to jump right into the hot tub without showering first. You would show yourself to be the ultimate *gaijin* (foreigner) and I shudder to think what would happen; it's the equivalent of peeing into a swimming pool. The most unusual aspect of the whole experience is that there is typically an elderly Japanese woman as the attendant in the bathing area, and it takes some getting used to. If she doesn't care, then neither should you; she's seen it all before. Once you get it through your head that this ritual is not some trick designed so everyone can stare at your private anatomy, the whole bath routine is a nice way to finish off your round, and does help your back feel better. Be warned, the scalding bathwater can lead to an unexpected contraction of that most important of organs.

Leaving the shower area, you put the slippers back on after you dress to walk back to your locker, but *only* after stepping out of the area with the baskets. It is hard to remember the precise choreography of all these steps since there are so many little nuances. The first time I did this whole routine I received some disapproving stares because I walked to the bath area wearing only my BVDs. Oops. At first, I thought the whole bathing ritual odd, but I came to enjoy it, and to this day it brings back very fond memories.

12. Have a post-round beer with your host. A post-round drink, usually beer, is customary and it is a good time to try to regain your dignity after the bath. At Naruo, we were sitting in the clubhouse attempting a couple of Japanese phrases in front of our host, butchering the language, when the server brought out a bowl of nuts and other munchies that looked to be pretzels. I popped one into my mouth and wished I could have spit it out—they were fish crackers wrapped in seaweed—but I sucked it up and told our host how delicious it was.

Because of the extensive rituals, the total time to play golf in Japan ends up being at least seven hours, from your pre-round coffee to your post-round drinks. Relax and enjoy the uniqueness of it.

The other characteristic I admire about Japan is the degree to which the society is so civilized. The taxi drivers wear a coat and tie and white gloves and their hospitality industry is genuinely service oriented. Upon arrival at your hotel the staff come out from behind the counter and bow, as do any staff nearby as you are getting into or out of an elevator. There is no tipping anywhere in the country; not in taxis, hotels, or restaurants. The Japanese are also unfailingly polite; they do not assume the person on the other end of the phone is deaf. In the week I spent in Japan, I only overheard one person speaking in a loud voice on a cell phone. They have one of the most civilized airports in the world, Narita, a fact that is even more impressive because the population of metropolitan Tokyo is the largest in the world, and twice the size of New York, with thirty-seven million people living there. Although one of the busiest airports in the world, you are treated as a human being instead of a cow; going through security takes ten minutes.

The conductor on the bullet train also impressed me; after he came through our car to punch tickets, as he was leaving he turned toward the passengers, bowed, and walked out backward, because apparently it's rude to walk out with people looking at your back. The Japanese transport system is so advanced it is a delight to be a traveling golfer. When you are finished with your round, the club asks where you will be playing next, and they have your clubs sent there for you for the equivalent of twenty dollars. It is a FedEx-type service that is nearly 100 percent reliable; you show up at the next course and your clubs are there, relieving you of the need to schlep them in your car, on the trains, or on planes. I also went to an inner-city, three-tiered driving range in Tokyo, which is a recommended experience and a good reminder of how lucky we are to live in such an expansive country.

I long to go back to Japan. It is such a unique country with such fabulous cultural rituals, although it can never be as good as my first visit, accompanied by my best traveling mate and a true Southern gentleman with an affinity for watermelons, Waffle Houses, and shrimp and grits.

South Korea

I have not played golf in Asia outside of Japan, and hopefully someday I will return. Aside from China, one of the countries on the rise with new courses that are gaining notice is South Korea. In 2001 the Club at Nine Bridges opened on Jeju Island, on the southern tip of the South Korean peninsula, between Japan and China. A private club, they tried to create the feel of a course in the Scottish Highlands, and it is known for its immaculate manicuring. Access is difficult, although I know four people who have played it by connecting with the club's general manager.

CHAPTER ELEVEN
"Private" Golf Courses

The entire book thus far has been focused on golf courses that are worth seeking out to play and range from resorts that welcome you to private clubs that are more—or less—difficult to access, depending upon their policies. This brief chapter looks at "private" clubs in the literal sense of the word. Wait until you see these courses, which were built for one individual or family for their private enjoyment and do not resemble traditional clubs. And I thought I was lucky being able to hit balls into the woods behind my house. Be prepared as you enter the sphere of billionaires.

Ellerston

Let's begin the exploration Down Under, at Ellerston, a course designed in 2001 by Greg Norman and Bob Harrison, which was built for Kerry Packer at his private estate in Scone, north of Sydney, in the Hunter Valley. Ellerston reportedly sees roughly ten rounds of golf *per week,* and the best characterization I have heard is it's a "bloke's retreat." Packer, a billionaire, was one of Australia's wealthiest people, who made his money in the media world. He owned a 70,000-acre estate and wanted Norman to build him a difficult course. Those that have played it describe it as severe and unrelenting. While he was alive, the invitation to play came from Packer himself.

Unlike almost any other course, I am at a loss regarding how to access Ellerston. Greg Norman describes the course as "extremely private" and apparently receives so many requests for access at his design firm's website that it contains the following message, "Greg Norman Golf Course Design cannot assist in booking tee times. Please contact the course directly with your inquiry." The course has not been ranked by any of the magazines I follow because not enough raters ever play it.

Apparently, Packer's son James now controls the invitations, but I have no idea whether this is true or not, as I have never been invited, nor have I tried. Ellerston remains an enigma.

Le Prince de Provence?

Built in 1991 and opened in 1999, Le Prince de Provence was originally a plan envisaged by the golfing Joneses, who purchased the land with some big ideas in mind. Conceived and designed by Robert Trent Jones and Robert Trent Jones Jr., the course is located in the French Riviera. According to Darius Oliver, who outlines the story in *Planet Golf*, the original plan was to develop a 2,500-acre property into three golf courses, a resort, and a housing development. Due to problems with the planning authorities, the course sat dormant for six years, although it was maintained to remain playable throughout that period. Due to the dispute with the French authorities it ran into financial problems and was returned to the bank that financed it. It was subsequently purchased by a syndicate of Norwegian businessmen who use it as their private golfing domain. *Bloomberg* wrote about the course in 2009 and identified Michael Hilti as the chairman of the club, and tells of how some people were blindfolded when taken there so they wouldn't know the exact location. The club's manager proudly told *Bloomberg*, "It's completely inaccessible. There are no sign posts, no marked gates, no website, and you won't find it on any global positioning system." Apparently they have more staff (thirty) than members (twenty-four). Although Darius Oliver refers to it as Le Prince de Provence, the course's name has been made intentionally unclear in the interest of throwing people off. When Robert Trent Jones was working on it, it was known as Vidauban. Whatever its name, it gets less than 500 rounds of golf per year.

Sanctuary

Designed by architect Jim Engh, Sanctuary, located in Colorado, is the private preserve of Dave Liniger and his wife Gail, who are the club's only members. The Linigers cofounded RE/MAX realtors and have done well for themselves. Although the course is for their private use, you can play it by attending a charity outing, which they allow multiple times per year, raising significant money for charities.

Sunnylands Estate

Billionaire Walter Annenberg, creator of *TV Guide,* was one of the earliest high-fliers to have his own private course—Sunnylands Estate, a 200-acre private enclave in the California desert. An immensely private place, the estate has a twelve-foot-high vine-and-shrub-covered fence around it. One of the privileges of such vast wealth is having the ability to create what you want. Annenberg's inspiration for building the course was his frustration in trying to book tee times to play around Palm Springs. The nine-hole course was built in 1964 by Dick Wilson; it was designed so it could be played twice, the second time around in a different configuration. Unusual twists along the way include a totem pole along the 5th fairway. Annenberg hosted seven presidents at Sunnylands: Ronald Reagan used to play there, as did Eisenhower, Richard Nixon, Gerald Ford, George H. W. Bush, Bill Clinton, and George W. Bush.

Sunnylands is owned today by a charitable foundation and trust, and their website is worth a visit if only to see the classic pictures of Ronald Reagan playing golf. The course can still be played, although you need an invitation from the family. I have never been invited, but President Obama visited and played in 2014.

Pocantico Hills

The Rockefeller estate north of New York City, Kykuit, overlooks the Hudson River. The estate has a private golf course, Pocantico Hills, which was originally a four-hole golf course built for John D. Rockefeller in 1899. It was expanded in 1901, and then in the 1930s William Flynn extended it to eighteen holes. It is a short course, playing only 5,673 yards. Although the course has eighteen holes, the design is unusual in that there are only ten greens, which are shared among some holes. Comparable to some of the packages you can buy from your phone provider, Pocantico Hills is for "friends and family" of the Rockefellers only.

Morefar Back O'Beyond

The name is a mouthful: Morefar Back O'Beyond Golf Club, and it is also in New York, not far from Pocantico Hills. Originally built and conceived as a retreat for the AIG Insurance Company, it was owned by the firm for a long time. It used to have only a couple of dozen golfers playing it per day, almost all for the purpose of entertaining clients. Before AIG's demise it was purchased by a former company executive, and it is still largely a mystery how to be invited.

The Billionaire's Playgrounds

Canada has become an appealing location for ultra-private golf courses with a host of "private" courses, including the Wildflower Golf Course in British Columbia, a nine-hole Robert Trent Jones Jr. design owned by Dennis Washington, a member of the *Forbes* 400. Another is Domaine Laforest in Quebec, which is owned by Canadian billionaire Paul Desmarais Jr. and run along the same lines as Ellerston. The American billionaire co-founder of McCaw Cellular, Craig McCaw, also has his own private Jack Nicklaus–designed course in British Columbia. Finally, there is "Goodwood," as it is unofficially called, built for oil man Gordon Stollery in Ontario. Although he passed away several years ago, his family still runs it as a truly private club.

Shifting back to the States, the nineteen-hole Porcupine Creek was built in the California desert by billionaire Tim Blixseth on a 249-acre estate and is now owned by Oracle billionaire Larry Ellison. There is also Houston businessman Jim Crane's Floridian course, which he purchased from billionaire Wayne Huizenga. Although it was originally used by the Huizenga family only, it now has a small membership and its own private helicopter service. Among other perks, the members enjoy private access to Tiger's former coach Butch Harmon.

"Private" and worth seeking out to play are not the same thing. It is hard to tell whether these golf courses are desirable or worth playing aside from the novelty of their ownership. I am not in a position to comment since I haven't played any of them. The long-term prospects for these courses remaining in private hands is dubious. What happens after the founder dies or when these courses move beyond the current owners? It is hard to tell, but for clues we can look to the past. At one time the Mellons, Vanderbilts, Henry Francis Dupont, and the Pratt Family—whose wealth came from Standard Oil—all had private courses, none of which remain private today.

Forward Progress

My journey continued in fits and starts over the years, with the universe of courses I set out to play gradually becoming smaller. It gets both easier and more difficult as you get near the end of a goal such as this. Easier, because as people see you getting nearer the finish line they are more inclined to help. More difficult, because as you exhaust all your contacts, new avenues to pursue to gain access become more scarce. As the end was approaching, I had three remaining courses left to play. Ironically, two were easy-to-access public courses on the Eastern Seaboard that I played as my ninety-eighth and ninety-ninth: the Homestead Cascades course in Hot Springs, Virginia, and Highlands Links in Nova Scotia. And then there was one remaining: Augusta National.

Before looking in detail at the methods you can pursue to play the course, there is one final fast-paced and inspirational story to share.

CHAPTER TWELVE

The Kiwi Miracle

It was a blue-bird day in the Sandbelt region of Melbourne. We were a content foursome, enjoying one of the top twenty-five courses in the world, the stylishly-bunkered Kingston Heath, and soaking up the abundant Australian sunshine. "Kia-ora" they said, using a traditional New Zealand greeting as they approached, two fit young lads in need of a shave and a few pounds. Little did I know that this

Wellington, New Zealand harbor.

serendipitous meeting would turn out to have such beneficial consequences over the years. As it turns out, Michael Goldstein and Jamie Patton were as golf-obsessed as I was; the two Kiwis were in Australia on their own golf quest. While my own personal odyssey stretched on for many years when I could gain access to a course or find the time, Michael and Jamie were trying to cram all their golf into a shorter time frame.

So, you are a couple of young lawyers sitting in your offices in Wellington, and are bored to tears with your chosen profession. We all have moments in our gray cubicles on a dreary day, doing some mind-numbing task and say to ourselves, "To hell with this, let's go out and play some golf." This is exactly what this young duo decided to do, but not simply for the afternoon. See, our two young lads think big. Very big. "Why don't we take the next year off and play golf every single day?" is what they actually said to themselves. On a different course. Around the world. With a minimal budget. Thus began what became "Puregolf 2010," and it encapsulates much of what I have

Paraparaumu Beach, Wellington, New Zealand, 8th hole.

been describing about how to play golf on some of the most exclusive golf courses into one story.

After quitting their jobs they launched a website and decided to raise money for charity along the way. A brilliant idea, and unhindered by family obligations and with a true spirit of adventure, they describe their trek on their opening blog post, "Puregolf2010 is a story about the Kiwi ethos. It was born out of a desire to challenge ourselves, and a challenge it certainly will be. But we're up for it. In 2010 we will play a round of golf at a different course every day of the year, around the world, to raise money for The First Tee New Zealand. Our journey starts on 1 January 2010 at Kauri Cliffs and will finish on 31 December 2010 at Cape Kidnappers. A calendar year, no less. In between, we will travel through New Zealand, Australia, and the United States, the United Kingdom, northern Europe, and parts of Asia. Perhaps other countries, too. Along the way we will play many of the world's best golf courses, meet a bunch of interesting people, and generally experience life outside our comfort zone. The plan is also to raise a significant amount of money, too. Puregolf2010, first and foremost, is an adventure. It embodies for us the truism that life is too short. Golf every day for a year . . . why not?"

Unlike most golf fanatics, who have an attention to detail that would make Felix Unger proud and believe the solution to everything in life is to build a spreadsheet, Jamie and Michael have a carefree spirit. Aside from mapping out a rough outline of where they would be and what courses they wanted to play, they mostly decided to take it day by day. They are agreeable characters and I immediately took a liking to them; their low-key styles and natural ability to tell stories drew me in. I met them on day eighty of their epic 365-day journey and told them I would be happy to host them when they came back to the East Coast of the United States. I put a nice post on my blog to help raise their profile, and, as is typical of golfers, who are a generous lot, they received several invitations to play when they came to the States, sight unseen. Who wouldn't want to meet two dashing, carefree, scratch-golfing Kiwis, show off their course, and be part of a dream year most people can barely conceive of? Maybe it was their charming accents, or the way they interacted and behaved, or because they were both clearly in need of a haircut, but the pair came across as

Kauri Cliffs, New Zealand, 5th hole.

a young McCartney and Lennon, a perfect match. My friends and I were the first Americans to meet them on their yearlong trip, and apparently we exceeded their expectations. In a post on their blog the next day they mentioned meeting us, and—probably because my friend Sheldon wasn't with us—noted that there were, "No grimaces; no swear words—just smiles." Is our reputation as Americans that bad? I know we have a bad image in some parts of the world, but come on, mates, we're not all foul-mouthed club throwers over here.

Once I was back home, I followed their blog postings each morning, which combined their impressions of the golf they played with entertaining observations and lots of local flavor. Each day I lived their adventure as if I were Walter Mitty in a secret life, fantasizing about being so carefree. One of the most impressive aspects of their journey was that they were doing it on a minimal budget, sleeping on people's couches where they could, getting their rounds of golf for free, and paying hosts back with nothing more than their *bon homie* and sharing their contagious, childlike sense of wonder. They had a knack for getting the media's attention, which didn't hurt in raising their profile and in propelling them forward to a new course each day. By the end of their journey, they were featured on New Zealand TV, in the *New York Post*, on the Golf Channel, BBC Radio, the *San Francisco Chronicle,* and Fox Sports in Australia, among other outlets. Through April they had already played an array of courses ranked among the best, including three renowned Australian ones: Royal Melbourne, Huntingdale, and Victoria in the Sandbelt region. Their momentum was building through their adroit use of technology and blogging, the media coverage they were receiving, and through the kindness of strangers.

Their self-imposed rule was to play at least one round of golf every day for the entire calendar year of 2010. They covered big parts of Australia and New Zealand in their early months, then took the big leap to the Northern Hemisphere. Their longest day was May 10, when they flew from Sydney to San Francisco, and due to the length of the flight they had to use their creativity to find a solution to play. In order to play on the 10th they teed off at 5:30 a.m. and played their round in a speedy ninety minutes. They ended the day on the campus of the University of California, Berkeley, where, of course, there was a protest in progress and they crashed on someone's kitchen floor. Their first purchase in the United States was a 1988 Dodge Ram Family Wagon with six-figure mileage on it that they nicknamed "Dodgy," as is the custom of those from Down Under, who seem to have an affinity for naming things. The plan was to sleep in Dodgy throughout their trek across the United States if they could find no other accommodation.

They started their United States journey with a bang and played the most prestigious courses in San Francisco in rapid succession: the Olympic Club, the San Francisco Golf Club, and the California Golf Club. It took me years and years to gain access to play at San Francisco and Olympic, and here the Kiwis were playing within a week of visiting the United States for the first time. As I have said repeatedly, having a good network of people, respecting the rules, and asking to be introduced to a member can sometimes be simple. They would politely ask and point out the charitable aspect of their journey, and their attitude was infectious to most people. Often there is an over-lap in the membership, or most certainly mutual friendships among members, which makes it relatively easy to network into the right clubs once the ball starts rolling. They had enough of a good start in the Bay Area that they kept building on it to keep their journey moving forward.

Their amazing feat and luck continued in Southern California, where they lined up Riviera, Bel-Air, and the Wilshire Country Club. Did I forget to mention they played the best golf course in the world when they were in Northern California? Indeed I did. Yes,

Cypress Point, 3rd hole.

they managed to play Cypress Point, which is about as difficult as any golf course in the world to play because of its small membership, Alister Mackenzie pedigree, and reputation as one of the most beautiful. As much as planning ahead and having the right connections to begin with helps, so does a large element of luck. As Thomas Jefferson famously said, "I am a great believer in luck, and I find the harder I work, the more I have of it," and the more time they worked at it and the more people they asked, the luckier they became.

As their journey continued east, their good fortune continued. If you were to list the greatest courses in New Jersey and Philadelphia they would include Merion, Pine Valley, Baltusrol, Somerset Hills, and the Plainfield Country Club. Jamie and Michael played all of them during their stay. Pine Valley, I remind you, is the number one ranked course in the world and golfers dream of playing it. I was happy to host them for a couple of days at my house and we played my home course, Hidden Creek, a Coore & Crenshaw design, where we stayed in the lodge overnight, traded stories, and emptied a bottle of single malt. We were having breakfast one morning before I was heading off to work and they were headed to Merion, and I asked them what their weekend plans were. "Bethpage Black on July 4th weekend," was their reply. I tried to explain how this might be difficult, as it would be more crowded than normal, and described how people lined up to play. In their typical Kiwi "why worry" style they said it would work out. During the middle of their stay, I had a previously planned trip to play at Sunningdale in England for a special occasion. As my wife and kids were away as well, I left them the keys to the house, asked them not to burn it down, and was on my way. After they left, they played at Winged Foot (of course they did, it's so easy to get on, no worries). As their luck continued, the pro at Winged Foot called the pro at Bethpage and was able to arrange a convenient tee time for them on the day they wanted to play. Luck begets luck.

They were asking many questions about where they should play in the Hamptons and I told them again how difficult I thought it would be; you can only laugh. Let's see, you want to play Shinnecock, the National Golf Links, Maidstone, and Garden City Men's in a week and you haven't arranged it yet? It's not going to happen. Unless you are a couple of charming Kiwis with an uncanny ability to network. It was to my utter amazement and joy that I read their blog posting of July 11th which they titled, "The

Greatest Day of Golf Ever Played." They played both Shinnecock and the National on the same day and had the lobster lunch! This doesn't happen in real life. For most people, it is hard to find a member and play *either* course, let along both of them on the same day. And, they managed to play Garden City, the Piping Rock Club, the Creek Golf Club, and the Westhampton Country Club.

One of my enduring memories of their journey is how their blog combined such whimsical humor with a good feel for what makes a dramatic juxtaposition. Thus, their pictures of Dodgy—custom painted in a design a pimp would love—parked outside the clubhouses of such venerable places as Winged Foot and Cypress Point tells the

Merion's historic 11th green.

story beautifully of how you do not have to be a member of the 1 percent to gain access to some of their playgrounds.

Their trip to the United Kingdom included a big chunk of the Open Championship Rota and other gems. To give a short list of some of the courses they managed to play: Kingsbarns, Prestwick, Royal Troon, North Berwick, Cruden Bay, Royal Dornoch, Muirfield, Carnoustie, Turnberry, Royal Lytham, Royal Liverpool, Royal Birkdale, and Royal St. George's. Mind you, they accomplished this on what can charitably be described as a low budget, with members hosting them or through the generosity of the club pros or secretaries' willingness to support the First Tee program. Throughout their journey they spent time with local First Tee chapters in New Zealand, England, and America, helping teach kids life skills and supporting the game.

Their ultimate prize in Great Britain was their ability to play Loch Lomond. As I have detailed, Loch Lomond is one of the hardest to play; as an international destination club, most of their members live outside Scotland. But, as was their destiny, someone they met in America knew a member and assisted them. See, it's not that difficult after all. Their luck continued throughout the British Isles. In Ireland they played a myriad of the best courses including Ballybunion and Waterville; around London they played Sunningdale and the appropriately named New Zealand Golf Club.

Their *pièce de résistance* was securing a round at Morfontaine. A feat that took me a sustained effort, they accomplished on short notice simply by continuing to ask everyone they met. In the ultimate act of selflessness, they had two open slots in their foursome and sent me an email asking if I wanted to play it again. One of my regular golfing companions had wanted to play Morfontaine for a long time, so on less than forty-eight hours' notice, we both rearranged our schedules, left our forlorn wives, eagerly used up frequent flier miles, and flew to Charles de Gaulle airport. What a day it was. Morfontaine was as outstanding as I had remembered it. We were immersed in the full French experience, had a lovely lunch in the idyllic clubhouse, with everyone straight out of central casting. The invitation illustrates how reciprocity works once you start on your journey to play these courses. Ask for nothing in return, expect nothing. We hosted the Fab Two because it was a treat and enjoying their company was all we expected in return. It feels good to help people on a quest. I have come to know some of their other hosts when they played in the States, and to a person they all said the same thing: we all benefited more by meeting them than they did getting a hosted round of golf. What happens when you give, is you get back. Nobody gets an email asking if they want to play Morfontaine, but I did, out of the blue due to their generosity, and was able in turn to help a friend. It is supremely ironic that we were invited to one of the most acclaimed, secluded, and difficult to access clubs in the world by an itinerant golfing duo with no standing at the club.

To my surprise and satisfaction, on my return visit to Morfontaine the extensive blog post I wrote about my initial visit was tacked up on a bulletin board in the manager's office. Apparently, he liked my in-depth and glowing review. What a turn of events, to go from a *persona non grata* to being highlighted within the club.

After leaving Europe, their amazing journey continued in the Middle East, and they ended up playing in Dubai with the Danish golfer Henrik Stenson, who was ranked number five in the world at the time. A difficult leg for them to pull off logistically was flying back to the Southern Hemisphere while still playing a round of golf every day. The best way to do it was to book an early morning flight from Dubai to Perth in Western Australia. Because of the length of the flight and the time change, they came up with an ingenious solution that only these two could have pulled off. They arranged for the Emirates Golf Club to light itself up at night with floodlights so they could play. They teed off at midnight, played a lightning fast round using golf carts, and finished by 2 a.m. With no travel hiccups, their ten-hour flight arrived in Perth on time and they played in a pro-am tournament with balls in the air at 11:30 a.m.

The Kiwis completed their quest on December 31, 2010, by playing Cape Kidnappers near Napier, New Zealand, to accomplish the impossible. Their journey is not something that is replicateable unless you have a strong back, can operate on little sleep, can spend an intense amount of time with another in close quarters without killing them, are a natural raconteur, have no shame in asking to play the best courses in the world on short notice, and have a liver that can tolerate your hosts buying you drinks every day for a year. But clearly, there are many lessons to draw, especially the power of networking, of using technology, of leveraging professionals to help you, of being lucky, of tapping into the right people; and how, once the ball starts rolling, momentum can carry you a long way. Once you find a member who plays at the San Francisco Golf Club, they introduce you to a member at Olympic who introduces you to a member at the California Golf Club, and on it goes.

When I met them back in April in Melbourne I warned them that getting access to private golf clubs in the United States was more difficult than it was in the United Kingdom or in Australia because they are so private. Boy, did I turn out to be wrong. The story of Michael and Jamie reinforces all that is good about golf, highlighting the generous fraternity of people that play this game, their ability and willingness to assist fellow golfers, the money that golf and golfers raise for charity, and the simple power of asking. In the end, they raised almost $40,000 for the First Tee and positively influenced many lives around the world, including mine. While they were not able to play Augusta, because they were in the United States during the summer when the course is closed, had it been open, I'm sure they would have somehow found a way to play it.

Their journey gave me a lesson in how to keep an open mind and to have a sense of adventure. Perhaps you do not need to incessantly plan everything? As they were fond of saying, "No worries, mate." Sometimes it just works out, as I was about to find out as I pursued my final course.

CHAPTER THIRTEEN
A Dozen Ways to Play Augusta National

After trying for almost a decade I managed to play ninety-nine of the top 100 golf courses in the world, and needed only Augusta to complete my quest. As you have seen, I ran into many obstacles over the years trying to play the course and I found it instructive to look at how people who have played the course managed it, to see if their techniques can be replicated.

As mentioned in the opening chapter, one of the most frequent questions people ask me is, "How did you get on Augusta?" And what they are in truth trying to figure out is if there is any long-shot way they may be able to play. My first reader poll on the blog was, "What is the hardest course in the United States to gain access to?" The overwhelming majority felt it was Augusta, with 63 percent agreeing it was the hardest, Cypress Point being the second most difficult.

Silly question, but would you go if invited? *Links Magazine* did a reader poll a couple of years back and asked the following, "You're on a business trip in Atlanta and have an important meeting that cannot be rescheduled. The night before the meeting, you receive a last minute invitation to play Augusta National Golf Club the following morning. What do you do?" Fifty-seven percent responded they would skip the meeting and play, 43 percent said they would attend the meeting. The 43 percent are out of their mind. Are you kidding me? Clearly, if you are reading this book you are not in the confused minority.

Augusta National entry gate on Washington Road.

So, how do you play Augusta? The best method is to play with one of Augusta's titans-of-industry members you know or are introduced to. As I have detailed, it is hard to do, especially since you can't ask. I have a vivid imagination and I always thought I would receive an invitation from one of the members I might be able to befriend through acquaintances. I had the visual image complete and replayed it over and over again in my mind. Driving to Teterboro Airport, flying down on their Gulfstream, having a 1982 Château Haut-Brion with dinner, staying in Eisenhower Cabin, watching old Masters reruns they show on the televisions in the cabins all night, playing thirty-six holes, and flying back without ever going through an airport security line.

For most people, there is an easy way to meet Augusta members, which is to go to the Masters, where they walk around wearing their impeccably-tailored green jackets. It was Cliff Roberts's idea to have members don them during the Masters so that if patrons needed to ask anyone for assistance they would be easily recognizable. Approaching them and asking to play is a bad idea, because: it's rude, it's an automatic no, and, you risk being kicked out of the tournament.

If I had to begin my journey again, I would collect five dollars every time someone told me they could help with Augusta through one of their connections—if I had done so my retirement would be fully paid for by now. Even though many told me they could help, until you put your tee in the ground and hit your shot down that enticing first fairway, it isn't over.

Two of my former New York colleagues had clients who were members and both had promised repeatedly they would try to help me, but it didn't come to fruition for several reasons. First, members do not play as much as you think they would; after all, they are successful, busy people and the course is only open six months a year. Second, as previously mentioned, many are elderly and do not keep up their games as much as someone who is young and vigorous might. And third, I don't think either of my colleagues liked me.

Mindful of the old adage about a management consultant being someone who knows 101 ways to make love, but doesn't know any women, I put together the following list of a baker's dozen possible ways to play fifteen months before I managed the impossible. For each of the methods I outlined, I made up odds with no particularly methodology, other than my skewed judgment. The methods are outlined below with the original odds I assigned:

1. **Begging and Hounding a Volunteer**

   Tom Clasby, who has played *every* course ever ranked in the top 100 finessed his way on in an unorthodox way. As he recounted to *Golf Magazine* in 2009, "The hardest is Augusta National by far! I got on because I was lucky enough to work the Masters as a fore caddie, which is almost equally impossible to playing the course itself. Some of the nicest, most understanding people helped, but it took five long years of begging and hounding everyone I ever met to get to these people."

   Odds of getting on this way: 5,000–1.

2. **Play With or For an Employee**

   Bernie Hiller of New York, who completed playing the world's top 100 in 1997, found his most difficult conquest was Augusta as well. As he recounted to the *New York Post*, "I'd finally almost finished the United States list, getting up to No. 99, but I could never get into Augusta," Hiller recalled. "I calculated that I talked to at least 5,000 people trying to get onto Augusta. Finally, I got to play Augusta. I played with the dishwasher.

It took me twenty years, seven months, and twenty-seven days from the time I first started trying to get on it."

Unfortunately, this technique can't be copied anymore because Augusta doesn't permit employees to bring guests or substitute another person for their once-a-year round. Alternatively, you could apply for a job and try to become a dishwasher, I suppose.

Odds of getting on this way: 1,000,000–1.

3. Work for a Broadcaster

One of my regular golf partners at home invited a guest to play with us one weekend and we started talking about all the courses we had played when I asked him if he ever played Augusta. "Augusta was the first course I ever played," was his nonchalant answer. His wife worked for *USA Network*, which at the time covered the Masters on Thursday and Friday. The course lets the television broadcasters play the Monday after the Masters, and he was at a dinner Sunday night and one of the golfers scheduled to play had to cancel. Although he had never swung a club before, the group convinced him it was the opportunity of a lifetime and he played. He laid some serious turf and shot over 150, but had an encouraging caddie and will forever be hated by every serious golfer who lusts to play Augusta and can't. The lesson in this is: aspire to become a senior executive of CBS. Or marry well.

Odds of getting on this way: 2,000,000–1.

4. Win the Bobby Jones Scholarship

This gem was submitted by one of my faithful blog readers, "I have played Augusta National. My secret? Attend St. Andrews University and win the Bobby Jones Scholarship to Emory University, which involves going to the Masters as a gallery guard in April and then going back to play the course in June, with full open clubhouse and unlimited use of the Par 3 course." Oh, to be young again and an athlete.

Odds of getting on this way: 10,000–1.

5. Do Nothing and Get "The Call"

Marc Brown completed playing the top 100 in the world for the first time in 1997. He has subsequently played all the courses on the biennially updated list between 1999 and 2009. His story: "Regarding Augusta, I got on the same way many average people do: purely by coincidence. About fifteen years ago, a seventy-year-old acquaintance told me that one of his friends was going to spend several days at Augusta, and he asked me if I would be available if a spot opened up. Several days later, an Augusta member called me and said that one of his guests had to leave town a day early and offered to let me take his spot. I scrambled to use Delta frequent flier miles since the round trip on three days' notice would have been over $2,000. I stayed overnight in a room above the golf shop, had dinner at Augusta, played one round and the par-3 course the next day, had lunch, and then left the premises, never to return except to watch a Masters practice round.

"Except for that one chance encounter with a seventy-five-year-old Augusta member (now deceased), I have not before or since had even the most remote opportunity to play Augusta National. My impression is that Augusta members are gun-shy about being asked to take guests that they do not know, and that they are more willing to take one stranger to fill a foursome than to take three strangers." Make sure to keep your cell phone charged.

Odds of getting on this way: 5,000–1.

6. Volunteer at the Masters

One of my hopes was that I could volunteer at the Masters and then play. My dream was to be assigned rope duty on the 15th hole and to stand there and watch approach shots into the green all day. Volunteers at the Masters play the course before it closes each May, which explains one of life's great mysteries: why the people who have pulled bathroom duty at the Masters are so cheerful. Wouldn't you be willing to clean toilets to get a chance to play Augusta? Alas, I tried this route to no avail. I sent a letter to the club in 2008. A couple of months later I received their reply, and, analogous to college applications, you know right away by the size of the envelope whether you were admitted or not. I was hoping for the thick packet and a nice welcome letter. I could tell by the thin nature of the envelope it was not good. To quote directly, "Dear Mr. Sabino: Thank you for your inquiry regarding volunteer work for the Masters Tournament. Your experience is certainly valuable; however, all our positions are filled and we cannot offer you any encouragement because the same volunteers return year after year—most serving for many years. Therefore, we maintain no waiting list." Period, end of sentence.

Odds of getting on this way: 2,500–1.

7. Win the Appropriate Amateur Championship

Finish first or second in the U.S. Amateur and you not only play Augusta, you get to play in the Masters, including all of its practice rounds, and to stay in the Crow's Nest—the cupola in the top of the main clubhouse. Likewise, the winner of the British Amateur gets an invitation, as does the U.S. Mid-Amateur champion and the current Asian Amateur champion. Golfer D. J. Trahan said his 2001 stay at the Crow's Nest was "indescribable." I'm sure it was.

Odds of getting on this way: 3,000,000–1.

8. Be Lucky

Selwyn Herson completed the top 100 in 2004. As told by *Travel & Leisure Golf Magazine,* "Herson's tour of the track Bobby Jones made famous fell from the sky. While doing some advisory work for a large communications company in New York, Herson was summoned to the office of one of the top executives. He thought he was in trouble, but the guy asked Herson to do him a favor, take his place in a group that was scheduled to play Augusta." Obviously he had spread the word beforehand that he wanted to play, which is imperative if you want to play at golf's Promised Land. He also told the magazine he was "goal-oriented." Just like me.

Odds of getting on this way: 2,500–1.

9. **Join Augusta Country Club**

    Augusta Country Club is the Donald Ross–designed course adjacent to Augusta National that is visible above the 12th green and 13th tee on Amen Corner. It is a separate, private club from Augusta National. Since Augusta National permits only foursomes to play, if, for some ghastly reason there aren't four golfers, Augusta National has been known to occasionally call over to Augusta Country Club to see if there's somebody hanging around that might want to drive over and join in at the Mother Ship. Standing by.

    Odds of getting on this way: 1,000–1.

10. **Be Invited by a Member**

    Being invited by a member is tough to do since its 300 members are dominated by an inner circle of America's current and former CEOs. In 2004, during the uproar over the club's all-male membership policy, *USA Today* published a list of members. More than 80 percent were current or retired CEOs of Fortune 500 companies. The average age was seventy-two; more than a few were in their eighties. There were many recognizable names on the list including Bill Gates, Warren Buffet, and former secretary of state George Schultz. Writing to them and asking won't work, but as Selwyn and Marc found out, members do invite people. Just not me.

    Odds of getting on this way: 5,000–1.

11. **Cover the Masters for the Media**

    There are twenty-eight members of the media allowed to play Augusta after the Masters concludes each year. Leonard Shapiro, who writes about golf for the *Washington Post*, wrote the following regarding his experience: "There is a media lottery every year, and it took me eight years to win a round the Monday after the Masters. By the way, for the ethicists out there, I paid the caddie $125 and spent another $200 in the pro shop, so there really is no such thing as a free round of golf for the sportswriters at Augusta National. By the way, had three pars on the card, four Xs, and had to walk off after fourteen holes to make a deadline, and then a plane." What kind of deadline could have been more important than finishing Augusta? This is difficult to understand. So you miss the deadline, are fired, and go to work for another paper. What am I missing?

Also, in the "not fair" category, Damon Hack from Golf.com won the lottery twice, in 2002 and 2009. Let's feel sorry for him, since he's not eligible to win the lottery again until 2016. Not.

The same courtesy is extended to vendors of the Masters, they are given a chance to play once a year on a designated day as well. Perhaps applying for a job with the company that makes the pimento-cheese sandwiches would work?

Odds of getting on this way: 1,000–1.

12. Become a Caddie

Similar to almost every course in the world, caddies at Augusta are permitted to play the course. But only once a year.

Odds of getting on this way: 5,000–1.

13. Play with a Past Champion

Even winning the Masters doesn't grant you automatic or regular access. Past champions are allowed one guest per year on the Sunday before the Masters begins. I told you it was hard.

Odds of getting on this way: Very long.

These were my original thoughts, and it turns out my odds-making abilities weren't too bad after all, as you'll see in the final chapter. I learned of additional methods subsequently, so before we move on to my own story of breaking through, I share them with you here. My blog readers are a learned group and I received a lot of feedback after publishing my thirteen methods. Shockingly, all my readers are not fans. One comment struck me as not particularly positive: "Making an obnoxious blog post . . . odds of getting on this way: Not going to happen." As you can see, I am a pathologically optimistic person and these negative messages always ended up giving me more motivation to succeed. One reason I decided to write this book was to show cynics they are wrong.

I mentioned in chapter three that the membership was old and a gentleman I met on a flight was sponsored but wasn't admitted because his sponsors died. In a similar vein, the following comment was left related to Augusta: "I once encountered a gentleman in Australia who befriended a visitor from Atlanta. The American was having a problem this fellow helped to sort out. They ended up playing golf together several times at the resort in North Queensland at which they both were staying and became buddies. At the end of the week, the American announced he was a member of Augusta and suggested his new friend was welcome to come any time and play as his guest. The Australian, being a gentleman, thought he should wait a decent interval before flying over. He phoned six months later to make the arrangements, only to be told the member had died!" As I said in the opening chapter, you need to be opportunistic and seize the moments when they come along.

A lucky Masters patron was in the right place at the right time during the final round of the 2012 Masters. Louis Oosthuizen made a double-eagle on the par-5 2nd hole, and after he picked the ball out of the hole, he was so giddy he tossed it to a patron. The patron was approached by an Augusta member—wearing his requisite green jacket—who asked for the ball for the club's archives because double-eagles are so rare (there have only been four in Masters history and Oosthuizen's is the only one that was shown live on television). The patron obliged, and what did he receive in return? Although the club would not confirm it, he played Augusta.

Apparently, there are more ways than meet the eye to get access. Another reader posted the following: "Employees for the local newspaper are permitted to play the

National on 'Augusta Chronicle Day' provided that they shoot 105 or better in a yearly employee tournament held in Aiken, SC. If too many people qualify, they draw names, I believe. But I think all newspaper employees are eligible, be they newsroom staff, advertising, press room, what have you. The *Chronicle's* owner and publisher, Billy Morris, has been an Augusta National member since the '60s." I could not independently confirm this, but if you were the *Chronicle,* would you confirm it to me?

There is one last way to get on Augusta, which is not widely publicized. Occasionally, rounds are auctioned off for charity. I know of one member in Connect-

Augusta National, 13th hole, "Azalea."

icut who auctioned off a round of golf for three which included riding down with him on a private jet. The cost was $12,000. Finally, Grandstand Sports based in New York assists charitable organizations in their fund-raising; at select auctions throughout the year they auction off a threesome at Augusta, and I'm told they have bidders about twice a year. Opening bid: $150,000.

CHAPTER FOURTEEN
The Holy Grail, Playing Augusta National

I shall never forget my first visit to the property ... The long lane of magnolias through which we approached was beautiful. The old manor house with its cupola and walls of masonry two feet thick was charming. The rare trees and shrubs of the old nursery were enchanting. But when I walked out on the grass terrace under the big trees behind the house and looked down over the property, the experience was unforgettable.

The paragraph above is a quote from Bobby Jones. His recollection is of seeing the Augusta National property before the course was built, and it is still apropos to this day. The famed football coach and Augusta member Lou Holtz once said, "I'm often asked to explain the mystique of Notre Dame. I reply, 'If you were there, no explanation in necessary. If you weren't, no explanation is satisfactory.'" The same is true about Augusta; it is hard to do justice to the experience in words.

Almost everyone has seen the course on television, and with high-definition especially, you can begin to appreciate the alluring nature of Augusta. Those that have been to the Masters can appreciate it even more, because they have seen first hand how perfect the entire property is. "Perfect" is a word that is easy to overuse. True perfection is rare. In the context of Augusta, though, it is not a figure of speech, it is a reality, since *everything* about the place is *literally* perfect. There are no weeds on the property and nothing is out of place. The club's obsession with perfection goes down to the tiniest details, including wrapping sandwiches sold at the Masters in green wrappers, so if one falls to the ground it blends in with the grass on television. It includes the hidden-from-view bathroom houses made of pine, used during the tournament, which are spotless, since nothing is beyond the club's consideration.

First-time visitors almost always say the same thing, that the steepness of the terrain doesn't come through on television, especially how much the 1st hole plays down and then up. Also, the uphill shots required on the approaches to the 9th and 18th holes are much more dramatic when seen in person; the latter hole has a seventy-three-foot rise—about the height of a six-story building—from the lowest point of the fairway to the green. The most dramatic hole of all, though, is the 10th, which is so monumentally steep people are usually stunned when they see it.

It took me ten years to receive the invitation to Augusta, but I finally managed to do it in style. When I created my list of a dozen ways to play I made it a baker's dozen, and it was a good thing. The thirteenth method was to be invited by a former champion, and that is how it happened. Some friends to whom I am forever indebted introduced me to a former winner and we got to know each other. When he learned what I was trying to accomplish he invited me out to play the day before the 2013 Masters. If his name wasn't redacted I wouldn't have revealed it anyway, because it is one of the nicest things anyone has ever done for me and my idea of paying him back doesn't include having him receive letters from legions of eager golfers asking for invitations to play. As I have said, it would not work; you need to be introduced.

For those of you who waded through the whole book in the hope I would tell you who it was exactly, my apologies. You should have been able to tell early on I was a fool, particularly when I gave you my feelings about the Old Course; you should have pitched the book right then and there.

After I was invited to play it took days for me to come back down to earth. Because I am a little anal and, clearly, I have an affinity for lists, I immediately began to keep three: 1) People who were previously my friends who told me they now hated me from jealousy; 2) People who offered to caddie for me, if needed; and 3) People who wanted "Augusta National" and not "Masters" logo items you can only buy in the pro shop in the clubhouse. Sleeping the night before playing was restless, at best (more like hopeless), the sense of anticipation, crushing. Sitting in my hotel room prior to leaving for the round, I was a clinical example of adult ADHD, and displayed all the symptoms in classic form: inattention, hyperactivity, and impulsiveness. I was babbling, moving papers around the room senselessly, and not listening to a word my patient wife said.

On the appointed day the weather was agreeable, about seventy-two degrees, with brilliant sunshine and the gentlest of breezes. I drove over from Atlanta with my generous host, who is one of the true gentleman of the game. He regaled me with his Augusta stories and how he managed to win the tournament, and all it means to him. As we pulled up to the club's gate off Washington Road, the guard stepped out and recognized him, and we were waved through. What better circumstances are there to play Augusta than as the culmination of a long quest, with the azaleas in bloom, when the course is in tournament condition, and with a Masters champion? Well, none.

I tried to finesse my way onto the course many different ways over the years, and in the back of my mind I knew there was always a possibility I would never play the course. Driving down Magnolia Lane is something I thought might never happen to me, and it would still have been an accomplishment to have played ninety-nine of the top 100 courses in the world, although since I had been to the Masters and walked the course, I would have considered it ninety-nine-and-one-half. I had surgery on my spine a year before playing, had gone into hibernation, and had stopped pressing. It was then that some extraordinarily generous friends introduced me unexpectanly to my future host. The range of emotions I felt being driven under the long canopy of trees was a full spectrum; the most prevalent feelings were joy, fear, excitement, disbelief, exhilaration, and anticipation.

Walking through the door of the plantation-style antebellum clubhouse is as memorable an experience as riding down Magnolia Lane. Having been to the Masters twice, I had already experienced the jaw-dropping awe of the property and its rolling hills. Not that it ever gets old, because it doesn't. Being anywhere on the verdant Augusta grounds is special, no matter how many times you have been there. This time, being able to walk into the clubhouse—an act previously forbidden—was profound, and I had the biggest smile of my life on my face when I entered.

As with everything else in this adult version of Disneyland, the interior of the stately clubhouse is flawless. It is the antithesis of glitz and ostentation; simple, elegant, and the ultimate embodiment of understated Southern charm. There are so many little touches they get right, including a mounted display board in the entry foyer; the board has slots that hold the engraved names of members who are currently on the property, and they slide brass name plates in and out as members arrive and depart. I was trying to act nonchalant and did my best not to gawk at the board, but recognized a couple of names, including their most famous female member, who was present. The clubhouse, with a two-story veranda around the entire building, was built in 1854. It is a veritable museum because it holds the permanent Masters trophy, historic golf clubs donated from past champions, and a sizable oil painting of President Eisenhower. Ascending the winding stairway leads you to the second floor, which contains the dining room where they hold the Champions dinner each year, and the Champions locker room.

The interior of the clubhouse is as perfect as the course. I am sure they don't paint it every week (right?), but the interiors of the buildings looked as if they were freshly painted. The flooring is polished, the carpets are spotless and look freshly laid, and the lucky people working there are charming and gracious. Inside the clubhouse they do not use an electric vacuum cleaner since the noise would disturb the reserved ambiance; instead, they use an old-school manual push-style that makes no noise. I received a tour of the entire grounds including each of the various buildings they use when they run the Masters. My distinguished player gave me a gift to remember the day by, a brand-new wedge made by Bob Vokey with my name engraved on it, and I put it into my golf bag without further thought. We warmed up on the driving range used during the Masters instead of on the member's driving range.

The former champions play from the back tees, as you would expect, but guests play from the member's tees, which play 6,365 yards. Because he is such a class act, my host was hitting off the members' tees with me on the 1st hole to make me feel more comfortable. Sir Nick Faldo and his son were teeing off behind us, and the three-time champion started to give us heat and suggested in jest to my partner they would be installing ladies' tees for him soon, since he couldn't handle the tournament tees.

I have obviously played many good golf courses and have teed off at some famous pressure-packed locales such as the Old Course at St. Andrews and at Merion with lunch in progress a few feet away. Hitting my first tee shot at Augusta was the most nerve-racking of all, and shortened both my breath and my backswing; my palms were sweaty and my stomach, full of butterflies. The first drive is over a big swale, and although the fairway is wide, the target area is not, since it narrows between the huge bunker on the right and the towering Georgia pines on the left. Looking back, it was one of the narrowest fairway landing areas on the course. Making contact with the ball on the first tee is harder than it sounds; having my tee shot go its normal distance down the fairway was a bonus.

I played well on the first five holes, then the gravity of the situation hit me and I fell apart for the next four or five. When we reached the 6th tee there were two teen-agers on the tee box and a couple of older gentleman sitting in a golf cart. My playing partner said they were people I should meet and he introduced me. One was Bob Goalby, who won the 1968 Masters, and whose name I recognized because he won in the famous incident when Roberto De Vicenzo was disqualified for signing the wrong scorecard. The other gentleman was Doug Ford, another winner. They were riding along in a golf cart with what I presumed were their grandkids as their guests, and they let us play through. As we walked back to the tee box I asked what year Doug Ford won, and it was 1957, five years before I was born. I pride myself on knowing golf history and know most of the old timers' names, even obscure names such as Horton Smith and Ralph Guldahl. I had just met a winner I didn't recognize, or if I did, thought was dead; but Doug was there, alive and kicking. And watching. As I set up to the ball, Goalby shouted over, "No pressure, only three former champions watching," and I pulled my tee shot left on the downhill 165-yard par-3.

I have since researched Doug Ford and found out he was born Doug Fortunato, and he is the oldest surviving winner of the tournament. His victory was come-from-behind, beating Sam Snead, and included holing out a shot from a plugged lie in the bunker on the 18th hole. In a happy coincidence, it turns out I played Augusta almost 100 years to the day my then–twenty-three-year-old grandmother emigrated through Ellis Island from Naples in April 1913, and it was nice to meet a fellow *paisano* at Augusta. America is the land of opportunity, and I am sure she could have never imagined her future grandson being in such an exalted place.

Just as all roads lead to Rome, all golf leads to the back nine at Augusta on a Sunday afternoon, and I was approaching the final holes of my long journey in just such a spot. The next hour was about to be one of the best in my life, and any golfer's dream.

I swung extra hard on the tee at the difficult 9th hole and pulled my drive so far left it ended up in the swale at the bottom of the hill, on the first fairway. My caddie and I walked down to play my shot and as we did he told me to wait up, someone was on the first tee about to hit, so we stood in the pinestraw between the holes and watched a ball sail by us down the first fairway. I had a good view of the 9th green and I lined up and hit the ball back to my hole. Who comes off the first tee as I am doing so, but Tiger Woods. He sees my playing partner and walks over to say hello. They talk for a few minutes and I am introduced, and he tells Tiger that today's round is the final one in my quest to achieve an obsessive golfer's Holy Grail. We exchange pleasantries and he congratulates me.

My body walks up to the 9th green, but my mind doesn't follow; it was still a thousand miles away as I was trying to comprehend meeting a golf icon. We putt out on No. 9 and walk to the 10th tee. We both hit our shots down the massive hill and are off to play the back nine. Except we're not.

The practice putting green is near the 10th tee at Augusta. Two-time winner José María Olazábal, who, at the time was the current victorious Ryder Cup captain, walks up to the tee and says, "Do you mind if I join you on the back?" My playing partner says, "No problem with me. John, Is it okay if he joins us?" What am I going to say? "No, I'm in a groove, why don't we continue as a twosome." The fairy tale continues.

I hit my drive on No. 10 as good as I could, and my ball was down the hill in the center of the fairway. Meeting Tiger and having José María join us was too much for me to take in and I started to lose it. My caddie was a veteran and helped me calm down; he told me it didn't matter how I played or what score I shot, to relax and enjoy it. Not that he was immune to it; he was shaking his head and said he couldn't believe what was happening either. I am an average golfer, with a fifteen handicap, and if there is one hope I had going into the round it was to play Amen Corner well. Due to the

Birdie putt, Augusta National, 11th hole, April 2013.

coaching from the caddie, I regained a sense of calm as I walked onto the 11th tee. Being able to hit the same shots the professionals hit is a dream every golfer has. One of the highlights of my life was hitting the middle of the par-4 11th green in regulation (the hole plays 400 yards from the member tees) with a shot that received a simultaneous "great shot" shout-out from two former tournament winners. My birdie attempt was captured by my alert caddie, who knew the gravity of the moment, and took the camera out of my golf bag without being asked. I rolled it to within six inches and was not disappointed with a tap-in par to start Amen Corner.

Standing on the par-3 12th tee I mentally blocked out the water, the ultra-shallow green, the bunkers in the front and in back, the azaleas, the television tower, and everything else. I adjusted for the one-club wind, visualized the shot, saw only the flag, and took a purposeful deep breath. I ended up hitting one of the best shots of my life, eight feet from the hole. This is the reason you stand on the range year after year and hit tens of thousands of practice balls—so when you need to, you can pull off the shot of your life, and it was satisfying. On No. 12 the member tees and the pro tees are in the same place, so I had the exact same shot they hit during the Masters, a 155-yarder over Rae's Creek. Walking over Hogan Bridge is something that cannot be described; it is as good as you think it will be, and a solemn, almost spiritual experience. My putt broke a good cup and a half, and when I heard it land in the bottom of the hole for a birdie, it was hard to absorb. I have had my ups and downs with my golf game over the years, but it was satisfying to birdie what Jack Nicklaus calls "the hardest hole in tournament golf." My host parred the hole and José María hit a high slice into Rae's Creek and ended up with a double-bogey. Not bad, beating two green jacket winners from the same tee box. Walking off the green, José María turned to me and said sarcastically, with a huge smile on his face, "You know John, you should stop showing off, you're making us look bad." If you were to imagine what hole you would want to birdie in the entire world of golf, this would be on the short list. Perhaps the par-3 16th at Cypress, the 17th at TPC Sawgrass, Pebble Beach's 18th, or the Old Course's Road Hole would come to mind too, but No. 12 at Augusta ain't bad.

I was one-under through two holes on Amen Corner, and hit a drive straight down the middle of the 13th fairway. I didn't so much walk over Nelson Bridge as I did float over it. My luck ran out when my ball rolled back off the 13th green and I took a bogey on the hole, but I was still overjoyed, having just lived a golf fantasy. When Herbert Warren Wind coined the phrase "Amen Corner," he described it as your second shot on the 11th, the entire 12th, and your tee shot on the 13th. In the original true sense of Amen Corner, I played it to near perfection.

I am blessed, and for some reason the golf gods were good enough to let me play respectably at Augusta. As is typical, I had my ups and downs. I hit my tee shot on No. 16 into the pond, pulled my ball through the Eisenhower Tree on the 17th, hit my fair

A picture you can't take as a spectator at the Masters: the 13th hole from the tee.

share of chip shots fat, and three-putted more than normal because the greens were tournament speed.

My biggest embarrassment of the day was on the par-5 15th hole. I hit a good drive left and laid up my second shot to about 100 yards. It is one of the many shots every golfer imagines hitting when they go to the Masters as a spectator. What club would you hit? Will you lay up or go for it? Will you play it safe or hit to the left side of the green? I laid up, and went for the left pin on my third shot. Sir Nick says, "The course is perfection, and it asks perfection." I hit it less than perfect and it rolled back into the first cut in front of the pond. We walked down to the green over Sarazen Bridge and I took out my brand-new Bob Vokey wedge and took a practice swing. I had to hit the ball straight up in the air to have any chance of holding the green, but it didn't look right when I set up to the ball, given the lie. I put the club back into my bag and took out my lob wedge. As I was taking my practice swing, the club slipped out of my hands and flew end-over-end into the middle of the pond in front of the green. Although everyone in my group thought it was funny, at the time I didn't see the humor in it, and was mortified. My lob wedge is now permanently a part of Augusta, laying at the bottom of those renowned murky waters. The only saving grace out of the incident was that it wasn't the new wedge.

The day was made extraordinary by getting to hear stories from my host and from José María about where and how they hit shots en route to their victories. On several holes, they dropped balls and showed me where they had to make putts from. After my last putt dropped on the final hole, I shook hands with two green jacket winners, and my journey across thirteen countries and twenty-three states, which included thirty-eight courses that have hosted significant tournaments, was done. I saved the best experience for last, and walking off the 18th green of Augusta as the last hole to complete my quest was the only way to finish. To say I was in a state of elation is a gross understatement. At that moment, and borrowing from Lou Gehrig's line, I was the luckiest man on the face of the earth.

To cap off the day-to-end-all-days I played the par-3 course and had a drink in the Champions locker room. It is small and intimate, with only three tables that seat four at each. The veranda outside the room overlooks the circular entry drive and Magnolia Lane. The room was full when I entered, and I was able to trade stories with a dozen former champions, just as you would in the grill room of your local club after a round. I saw my buddy Doug Ford again in the locker room, told him about my birdie and found out he birdied the 12th on Sunday en route to his victory as well. The players were down-to-earth and we talked about the same types of things you talk about after a round with your friends: how poorly you putted or chipped, which holes you played well, et cetera. It was the crowning achievement of my long and very satisfying journey.

The only way the day could have been any better would have been if Chairman Billy Payne came out of a hidden doorway holding a golden chalice, showed me the secret handshake, and offered me a membership. Aside from my minor fantasy, Hollywood couldn't have scripted it any better.

So how is the course to play for an average player? From tee to green there is no rough, so putting your ball in play is not hard. The fairways are generous, they look and feel like carpets, and every lie is perfect. The greens are perfection, no-holds-barred the best in the world. The most difficult shots tee to green are those you have to hit off of pine needles if you are not in the fairway. The real tests at Augusta are chipping, holding your ball on the greens, and putting. The greens are fast, as you would expect. They are significantly harder on the back nine, in my humble opinion. In particular, I found the 13th, 14th, 16th, 17th, and 18th to be similar to putting on the top of a glass table. The players think the 11th is the hardest hole, but since I parred it, I think it rather easy. Personally, I thought the 7th was the hardest because it is tree-lined and plays to an elevated, well-bunkered green that is more uphill than it looks. My favorite hole on the course was the 13th; it is breathtaking and on a scale most golf holes can never achieve. The back tee is one of the most peaceful places in the world and sits in a little alcove in the back of Amen Corner; standing there, one has not a care in the world.

I have a big imagination. You have to, to envision playing Augusta and completing this quest. My experience at Augusta exceeded anything I could have ever imagined. Any one of my experiences that day are remarkable in their own right. Are my descriptions of Augusta hyperbole? Not in the least, when you experienced what I did as the culmination of a long journey and finish at the best place of all.

Many heartfelt thanks to the caddies who helped me stay calm and in the present, and let me enjoy the moment; and to the greatest champion the Masters has ever known, who is a prince of a human being and a true gentleman. And, to my Southern friends who went out of their way to help me play Augusta, I am eternally grateful, especially Suzanne and James. It would be wrong of me to write a book and not put in at least one "Roll Tide" to honor you, my friend.

As you have seen, I have played in some spellbinding and memorable places. My day at Loch Lomond was exceptional, my experience and the ambiance of the cozy lodge at Morfontaine is still something I think about all the time, visiting Tasmania to play golf should be on everyone's bucket list, as should playing Cypress Point; it is also hard to beat an overnight stay at the National Golf Links. Yet, this is the one to tell the grandkids about (some day).

I am often asked what I will do now that I have completed my quest. The truth is I have no further golfing goals to conquer, no more mountains to climb. The whole day at Augusta was one overwhelming experience after another. Nothing I do in the world of golf can be more thrilling than the way it ultimately played out. As I have said, I am a believer in fate and there was a reason I was turned down so many times in my attempts to play Augusta. How could I have known that providence kept intervening so that I could finish with the best ending imaginable? And, so the best wife and mother in the world could come along and experience it with me.

The greatest round of golf I ever played was not at Augusta, but on my home course, during a lazy summer twilight round, eleven years before, with my kids when they were eight years old. We were playing as the sun was setting, and few people were out on the course. They were having as much fun driving the golf cart as hitting the shots and we were laughing and having a grand old time. I have a large collection of scorecards from all the courses I have played around the world, but none is more precious to me than the one written in their handwriting with the big scores on it. I have always tried to keep two hands firmly on the wheel, to keep the important things in life in perspective. These accomplishments would not mean anything to me if I didn't have a healthy and loving family.

As the existential philosopher said, you do not necessarily understand your life at the time you are experiencing it, but you can figure out the true meaning by reflecting back on it. My journey began as a quest to play a list of golf courses. Going in, I didn't understand what it would turn into or what I was doing. It ended up being not about the golf courses but about making new friendships, strengthening old ones, and enjoying the camaraderie of some great people. Pursuing this alone would have been no fun at all. Ultimately, it was all about the anticipation, the challenge, the shared experiences, the laughter, and the journey itself. I learned that life's purpose is to be with and enjoy your family and friends, to appreciate what you have, and to give back to others. Many people have been unstinting in their generosity to me, and I plan on continuing to help others achieve their dreams. Since there is no way for me to pay everyone back for their generosity, my plan is to continue to pay it forward, as the expression goes.

The real secret about Augusta is that it is easier for Southerners to play. After all, Augusta is a private club located in the South, and more members are from that region than any other. Although there are a lot of well-known members, there are many hardcore folks from Dixie, and connecting with them is easier for Southerners than for everybody else. So my final advice if you want to play the course is to focus on your Southern connections, and I wish you good luck and Godspeed in pursuing your own dream. I have had no regrets pursuing mine.

Twenty years from now you will be more disappointed by the things you didn't do than by the ones you did do. So throw off the bowlines. Sail away from the safe harbor. Catch the trade winds in your sails. Explore. Dream. Discover.

—Mark Twain

SECTION III
Appendices, Bibliography, & Index

Appendices

Summary of Methods
to Access the Golf Courses

1. Find a member and ask
2. Stay at a resort or the right hotel
3. Arrange to play in advance in the British Isles, Australia, New Zealand, and South Africa
4. Leverage your golf professional
5. Use technology (blog, email, newsletters, Google Alerts)
6. Play in a charity auction
7. Join a specialized club that provides access to a wide range of clubs
8. Ask a course owner
9. Ask a course architect
10. Network with a greenkeeper/superintendent or member of the staff
11. Camp out overnight at Bethpage
12. Join a golfing society
13. Volunteer at a PGA event
14. Play in a pro-am
15. Become a rater for a golf magazine
16. Become a caddie
17. Become a golf journalist
18. Go to Harvard or Yale
19. Get a good golf tour provider
20. Work on Wall Street or for a consulting firm

21. Call the course and ask to play
22. Play in the Tiger Woods Charity Playoffs
23. Do nothing and wait to be asked
24. Get a "peg" board
25. Leverage a corporate membership
26. Join the diplomatic corps
27. Meet a member of The Links
28. Join a top club for reciprocity
29. Subscribe to a newsletter that can provide tips
30. Bring a "letter of introduction"

How I Managed to Play
at Each of the Clubs

In total, I used eighteen different methods to access all the clubs I wanted to play. Some are listed more than once because I have been lucky enough to play more than once. The numbers written in parenthesis represent the club's world ranking at the time I was trying to play using the *Golf Magazine* 2003 ranking.

Direct invitation from a member
Pine Valley (1)
National Golf Links of America (20)
Inverness (58)
Maidstone (60)
Peachtree (87)
Paraparaumu Beach (99)
The Links
Myopia Hunt Club
Whippoorwill Club

The majestic entry drive, Myopia Hunt Club, Massachusetts.

Unaccompanied guest through an introduction to a member

Cypress Point (2)   Congressional (86)

Medinah (52)   Yeamans Hall (92)

Followed their booking procedure for guest play

Muirfield (3)   Portmarnock (40)

Pebble Beach (7)   New South Wales (43)

Royal Melbourne (8)   Sunningdale Old (44)

Pinehurst No. 2 (9)

Royal County Down (10)

Royal Portrush (12)

Ballybunion Old (13)

Royal Dornoch (16)

Turnberry Ailsa (17)

Pacific Dunes (19)

Kingston Heath (21)

Carnoustie (26)

Royal Birkdale (28)

Bethpage (30), with a New York resident

Royal St. George's (32)

Casa de Campo (34)

Royal Troon (38)

Prestwick

North Berwick

Valderrama (77)

Kiawah Island Ocean (79)

Walton Heath (82)

El Saler (93)

European Club (98)

Barnbougle Dunes

Jack's Point

Woodhall Spa (46)

Kauri Cliffs (49)

Royal Adelaide (50)

Whistling Straits (53)

Royal Lytham & St. Annes (54)

TPC Sawgrass (57)

Ganton (62)

Highlands Links (64)

Kingsbarns (65)

Harbour Town (67)

Cabo del Sol (68)

Durban (70)

Royal Liverpool (72)

Lahinch (73)

Bandon Dunes (74)

Cruden Bay (76)

Wentworth West (78)

Spyglass Hill (81)

Walton Heath Old (82)

World Woods (83)

Homestead Cascades (94)

Machrihanish Old

Kingsbarns, St. Andrews, Scotland, 3rd fairway.

Greenkeeper
Shinnecock Hills (4)
National Golf Links of America (20)

Former Masters winner
Augusta National (5)

Tee time booked through hotel
Shadow Creek (89)
Mid Ocean Club

Old Course Experience package
Old Course at St. Andrews (6)

Architect
Sand Hills (11)
Friar's Head

Introduced to a member & played with them	Degrees of separation
Merion (14)	2
Oakmont (15)	2
Winged Foot West (18)	2
Seminole (22)	3
Oakland Hills (25)	3
San Francisco (26)	3
Fishers Island (29)	3
Chicago Golf (31)	3
The Country Club, Brookline (33)	4
Riviera (36)	3
Olympic Lake (39)	3
Baltusrol (45)	2
The Golf Club (48)	3
Shoreacres (51)	3
Garden City (55)	3
Loch Lomond (56)	4
Los Angeles North (59)	2
Camargo (63)	4
Winged Foot East (66)	3
Somerset Hills (69)	3
Ocean Forest (84)	4
Valley Club of Montecito (85)	2
Wade Hampton (88)	4
Cherry Hills (90)	4
Hyannisport Club	2
Sebonack	2

Shoreacres Dining Room, Lake Bluff, Illinois.

Through a custom tour operator
Hirono (35)
Naruo (75)
Kawana (80)

Corporate membership
Muirfield Village (37)
East Lake (97)

Through a PGA professional (club pro)

Prairie Dunes (23)
Southern Hills (41)
Scioto (71)
Colonial (100)

Charity outing

Oak Hill East (42)
Bethpage Black (30)
Maidstone (60)

Unaccompanied guest through introduction to someone who knew a member

Morfontaine (47)   Degrees of separation: 5

Prairie Dunes, Kansas, 2nd hole.

Unsolicited invitation via my blog

Quaker Ridge (61)

Baltimore Five Farms East (91)

St. George's (95)

The Honors Course (96)

Tokyo Golf Club

Called the course and asked

Crystal Downs (24)

Waited in line in the morning

The Old Course at St. Andrews (6)

Invited by two itinerant Kiwis (do nothing and wait)

Morfontaine (47)

Still waiting

Royal & Ancient Golf Club of St. Andrews

East Lake Golf
Club, Atlanta.

My Ideal Composite 18-Hole Course

An ideal composite is a compilation of a hypothetical golf course based on the "best" holes from a variety of different courses.

1. Prestwick, Par-4, 346 yards — It's short; but the history, stone wall, & railway make it ideal

2. Pine Valley, Par-4, 388 yards — Deceptively narrow, huge uphill second shot, severe green

3. Durban, Par-5, 468 yards — Par-5 in a valley, surrounded by bush

4. Morfontaine Valliere, Par-3, 150 yards — Downhill par-3 in a sea of heather and fern

5. Mid Ocean, Par-4, 433 yards — Cape hole. Impossible to hit the fairway into the wind?

6. Sunningdale (Old), Par-4, 386 yards — The best use of cross-bunkers I have seen; a walk in the park

7. Sunningdale (Old), Par-4, 393 yards — Blind, dogleg, elevated green, scenic; near perfection!

8. Prairie Dunes, Par-4, 430 yards — Uphill all the way on this dogleg right; wavy fairway

9. Maidstone, Par-4, 415 yards — Between the dunes and the Atlantic, no weakness anywhere

Front nine: 3,409 yards, par 36

10. Riviera, Par-4, 315 yards — The definition of risk vs. reward; short par-4s are easy?

11. Merion, Par-4, 367 yards — Tricky short par-4 that Bobby Jones won the Grand Slam on

12. Augusta National, Par-3, 155 yards — 155-yarder over Rae's creek, narrow green, well trapped

13. Augusta National, Par-5, 510 yards — The single best golf hole in the world?

14. Baltimore Five Farms, Par-5, 570 yards — A brilliant Tillinghast par-5 on great terrain

15. Cypress Point, Par-3, 135 yards — The sexiest hole in golf, par-3 in an alcove

16. Cypress Point, Par-3, 222 yards

The most heroic par-3 in golf, 200+ carry over water

17. National Golf Links, Par-4, 375 yards

Peconic. Play it once before you die

18. Pebble Beach, Par-5, 543 yards

Sometimes the hype is true; it certainly is here

Back nine: 3,192 yards, par 36

Total: 6,601 yards, par 72

Baltimore Country Club, Five Farms Course, 14th hole.

Like me, the scorecard is a bit unbalanced with the front playing nearly 300 yards longer than the back.

The total yardage is a respectable distance, especially considering the fact that I have several shorter risk-reward par-4s included. I am not a big fan of length and think the game is better played with brains rather than brawn. Hole ten proved to be my biggest dilemma. It is hard to beat Riviera's 10th, which nicely proves my thesis that golf holes do not have to be long to be hard, but, Sunningdale's Old Course and Royal Melbourne West were close seconds for a 10th. Other close calls were Carnoustie's and Durban's 17th, The National Golf Links' 16th, and Jack's Point's 15th. National Golf Links 8th Bottle hole was also a close call.

I hope I didn't break any ideal/eclectic course rules by using three sets of back-to-back holes from Sunningdale, Augusta, and Cypress, and two sets of back-to-back par-3s and 5s (for permissibility study Cypress Point, which has both). The designer who ended up with the most holes in my eighteen was Alister MacKenzie.

My Personal Top Fifty Clubs in the World

If you could play just one course, what would it be? For me it is Cypress Point. For Ben Hogan, the one course he said he could play happily for the rest of his life was Seminole. Tom Lehman wrote a letter to Shinnecock Hills in 1995 stating, "If I were given one day to live, and could play any course that I wanted for my last round, I would choose Shinnecock." If you had unlimited time and money and access to whatever courses you wanted, which courses would you put on your short list to play? (We have already established that I can't add.)

Shinnecock Hills, Southampton, New York, clubhouse.

Top 10

Cypress Point
National Golf Links of America
Sand Hills
Carnoustie
Loch Lomond
Sunningdale (Old)
Cruden Bay
Maidstone
Pine Valley
Royal Adelaide
Merion
Morfontaine
Augusta National

Second 10

Shinnecock Hills
Camargo
Shoreacres
Royal Portrush (Dunluce)
Yeamans Hall
Jack's Point
Royal County Down
Woodhall Spa
Barnbougle Dunes
San Francisco Golf Club

Woodhall Spa, England, 12th hole.

Third 10
Turnberry
Whippoorwill Club
Los Angeles Country Club
Seminole
Somerset Hills
Royal Melbourne West
Kauri Cliffs
Kawana
Bethpage Black
Kingsbarns
Yale

Fourth 10
Pebble Beach
Riviera
Crystal Downs
Prestwick
New South Wales
Baltimore (Five Farms)
Highlands Links
Garden City Men's
Naruo
Myopia Hunt Club

The Last 10
Bandon Dunes
The Valley Club of Montecito
Lahinch
Pinehurst No. 2
Royal Dornoch

Hirono
Chicago Golf Club
Valderrama
Royal St. George's
Cabot Links

The dining room at Morfontaine.

The Best of the Best

Mirroring Tom Doak's Confidential Guide Gazetteer, this section focus on only one aspect of a club. Sometimes it is difficult to separate the course from the club, location, and traditions, so we look at one criteria at a time.

The Best Views and Awe-Inspiring Locations

- Augusta National
- Bandon Dunes
- Barnbougle Dunes
- Cape Kidnappers
- Cypress Point
- Jack's Point
- Kauri Cliffs
- Kawana
- Kingsbarns
- Loch Lomond
- New South Wales
- The National Golf Links of America
- Old Head of Kinsale
- Pacific Dunes
- Pebble Beach
- Royal County Down
- Sand Hills
- Turnberry

New South Wales Golf Club.

The Most Historic

- Augusta National
- Ganton
- Garden City
- Merion
- Muirfield (The Honourable Company of Edinburgh Golfers)
- Myopia Hunt Club
- The National Golf Links of America
- North Berwick
- Oakmont
- The Old Course at St. Andrews
- Prestwick
- Royal Liverpool Golf Club
- Royal St. George's
- The Country Club

Myopia Hunt Club, 18th fairway.

A Unique Experience, You Will Remember Visiting and Playing for a Long Time

- Augusta National
- Cruden Bay
- Cypress Point
- Durban
- Fishers Island
- Morfontaine
- Muirfield (The Honourable Company of Edinburgh Golfers)
- The National Golf Links of America
- Pine Valley
- Shadow Creek
- Yeamans Hall

Special Places in Total, Taking into Account All Aspects of the Experience and the Course

- Augusta National
- Camargo
- Cypress Point
- Los Angeles Country Club
- Maidstone
- Merion
- Morfontaine
- The National Golf Links of America
- San Francisco Golf Club
- Somerset Hills
- Sunningdale
- Yeamans Hall

Clubs I Would Want to Join

- Camargo
- The Links
- Maidstone
- Myopia Hunt Club

Camargo, Cincinnati, Ohio, 1st hole.

- Royal Liverpool Golf Club
- San Francisco Golf Club
- Shoreacres

- Somerset Hills
- Sunningdale
- Yeamans Hall

The Best Hotels I Stayed at on the Quest

- Udny Arms (Cruden Bay)
- Dower House Hotel (Woodhall Spa)
- Lochgreen House (Royal Troon & Loch Lomond)
- Greywalls (Muirfield)
- Charleston Place (Yeamans Hall)
- Four Seasons George V

- (Morfontaine)
- Westin Valencia (El Saler)
- Westin Sydney (New South Wales)
- Sea Island Lodge (Ocean Forest)
- 88 Lodge (Kauri Cliffs)
- The Marriott Courtyard (Augusta, Georgia)

The Hardest Courses

- Bethpage Black
- Naruo
- Oakland Hills
- Oakmont

- Olympic (Lake)
- Pine Valley
- Royal County Down

The Best Clubhouses

- Augusta National—The former plantation house has no equals
- Camargo—Understated elegance
- East Lake—A shrine to Bobby Jones
- Garden City—A museum
- Loch Lomond—Rossdhu House, most grandiose
- Morfontaine—Cozy French hunting lodge
- Myopia Hunt Club—New England perfection
- National Golf Links of America—Like a London gentleman's club
- Oakmont—Golf mecca, old-style, old-world charm
- Royal & Ancient Golf Club of St. Andrews—The home of golf
- Royal Liverpool—Traditional English, warm and inviting

- Seminole—Pink, just like my favorite shorts
- Shoreacres—Up on a bluff overlooking the lake, classy and classic
- Sunningdale—The Stockbroker's Tudor
- Winged Foot—Elegant stonework in a grand setting

Captains, Royal Liverpool Golf Club, England, Dining Room.

The Best Caddies

- Augusta National
- Carnoustie
- Cypress Point
- Pine Valley
- Prestwick
- Royal Dornoch
- Royal Portrush

The Best Driving Ranges

- Augusta National
- Kauri Cliffs
- Pine Valley
- Tokyo's inner-city, multi-tier ranges

Best Conditioned Greens

- Augusta National
- Camargo
- Carnoustie
- Merion
- Peachtree
- Pine Valley
- Winged Foot

Winged Foot, East Course, 13th hole.

Best Food Along the Way
- In-and-Out Burger (California)
- Lobster lunch (National Golf Links of America)
- Old-school lunches (Royal St. George's and Prestwick)
- Sticky Toffee Pudding (Udny Arms near Cruden Bay)
- Sip 'N Soda (Breakfast before Shinnecock or National. Cash only)
- Ginger Snaps with Peanut Butter (Somerset Hills)
- Ginger Snaps without Peanut Butter (East Lake)

Favorite Architects
- Charles Alison
- H. S. Colt
- Bill Coore & Ben Crenshaw
- Perry Maxwell
- Charles Blair Macdonald
- Alister MacKenzie
- Willie Park Jr.
- Seth Raynor
- Tom Simpson

Underrated Courses
- Bandon Dunes
- Camargo
- Carnoustie
- Cruden Bay
- Kawana (Fuji)
- Kingsbarns
- Naruo
- National Golf Links of America
- Royal Liverpool (Hoylake)
- Sunningdale (Old)

Courses that Should Be on the Top 100 list
- Chantilly, France
- Jack's Point, Queenstown, New Zealand
- Myopia Hunt Club, South Hamilton, Massachusetts
- North Berwick, Scotland
- Old Head, Kinsale, Ireland
- Prestwick, Scotland
- Whippoorwill Club, Armonk, New York
- Yale, New Haven, Connecticut

Best Opening Holes

- Durban 1 through 5
- Highlands Links 1 through 8
- Merion
- Prestwick
- St. Enodoc
- Spyglass Hill 1 through 4

Best 9-hole Course

- Morfontaine Valliere

Best Finishing Holes

- Carnoustie 16 through 18
- Cypress Point 14 through 18
- National Golf Links of America 16 through 18

Worth the Trip

- The Playboy Mansion off the 13th green at Los Angeles Country Club
- Monkeys on the course at Durban Country Club
- Nude sunbathing on the adjacent beach at El Saler
- Outside traction system for clubs and escalators for players add to Naruo's allure
- Standing on the first tee at the Old Course at St. Andrews
- The nineteenth-century and regal feel of Myopia Hunt Club, especially when the riders and hounds are out
- Traveling to Tasmania to play Barnbougle Dunes
- Visiting the South Island of New Zealand, Queenstown, and Jack's Point
- Walking in JFK's steps at Hyannisport Club, next to the Kennedy compound
- Seeing Cruden Bay for the first time
- The long and winding drive to Machrihanish

Best Entry Drives

- Augusta National
- Cape Kidnappers
- Kauri Cliffs
- Morfontaine
- Myopia Hunt Club
- National Golf Links of America

- Sand Hills
- St. Enodoc (the hedge roads of Cornwall)

- Yeamans Hall

Best Halfway Houses
- Maidstone
- The National Golf Links of America
- Pine Valley

- Shoreacres
- Sunningdale

Hardest Walks
- Bethpage Black
- Highlands Links
- Naruo
- New South Wales

- Olympic Club
- Wentworth West
- Yale

Friar's Head, Long Island, 15th hole.

Best Walks—"Wow" Moments

- Augusta National—Driving down Magnolia Lane
- Augusta National—The approach to Rae's Creek on the 11th hole
- Augusta National—The walk from the 12th tee to 12th green, over Hogan Bridge
- Augusta National—The walk from the 13th tee to 13th fairway, over Nelson Bridge
- Barnbougle Dunes—The walk from the 4th green to 5th tee
- Cypress Point—The walk from the 14th green to 15th tee
- Cypress Point—The walk from the 15th green to 16th tee
- Fishers Island—Walking over the hill and seeing the "Punchbowl" 4th green
- Friar's Head—Walking up the "Stairway to Heaven," 14th green to 15th tee
- Highlands Links—The half-mile walk from the 12th green to the 13th tee
- Jack's Point—Looking over the wall and seeing the 15th hole
- Kauri Cliffs—The walk from the 7th green to the 8th tee

St Enodoc, Cornwall, England, 1st green.

- National Golf Links of America—The walk from the 16th "Punchbowl" green to the 17th tee
- Pebble Beach—Walking up the 18th fairway
- Pinehurst No. 2—Walking down the 1st and 2nd fairways
- Royal County Down—Looking at the vista on the 9th fairway
- St. Andrews—Walking across the Swilcan Bridge and up the 18th hole
- St. Enodoc—Walking up and over the hill to the 1st green

Best Rituals
- Muirfield's pomp, lunch, and alternate shot after lunch
- Bath after round, Japanese Golf (Naruo, Tokyo, and Hirono)
- Sand Hills overnight stay in the middle of nowhere

Other Unique Elements
- North Berwick's stone walls
- The hangman's noose at the Golf Club (Ohio)
- Outdoor escalators at Hirono and Kawana
- The elevator at Bel-Air
- Playing in "the bush" at Durban
- Hitting over the hedge row at Cypress Point's first hole
- Pine Valley's self-enclosed township

Golfers Who Have Played the Top 100 Courses in the World

1. James A. Wysocki (1986) of Louisiana, the first man ever to do so!
2. Robert McCoy (1988) of Florida and Massachusetts
3. Norman Klaparda (1993) of California
4. Samm Klaparda (1998), the first woman to have played all 100
5. Oliver "Bud" Thompson (1995) of Ohio
6. James Dunne III (1995) of New York
7. Rich Hoover (1997) of Pennsylvania
8. Bernie Hiller (1997) of New York
9. Mel Hughes (1999) of Colorado
10. Rod Boren (2000) of Ohio
11. Sunil Kappagoda (2000) of New York
12. Selwyn Herson (2004) of California
13. Alan Heuer (2004) of Connecticut
14. Leon Wentz (2005) of California
15. Randy Pace (2006) of Florida
16. Dick Michaux (2006) of California
17. Marc Brown (2007) of California (all courses on lists from 1999–2011)
18. Quentin Lutz (2007) of Ohio
19. Tom J. Clasby III (2009) of California (completed every course ever ranked in the top 100!)
20. Masa Nishijima (date unknown) of Japan
21. Mark Lampert (2010) of North Carolina
22. Bill Schulz (2012) of Arizona (all courses on lists from 2001–2011)
23. John Sabino (2013) of New Jersey
24. Erlend Malfait (2013) of Belgium
25. Paul Rudovsky (2014) of North Carolina and Massachusetts (working toward playing every course ever ranked in the top 100 worldwide)
26. Hong-Seh Lim (2014) of California (all courses on the list from 2003–2013)

27. Michael J. Durham (2014) of Texas
28. Larry Nicholls (2015) of Nevada
29. Fergal O'Leary (2015) of Ireland
30. Jonathan Orszag (2015) of New York

* Ralph Kennedy of New York gets an honorable mention

Acknowledgements

My first ever round of golf was with one of the true rummies of the game, Tom Trillo. I am forever grateful to you for introducing me to the game. I have learned a lot from you about what is important in life and how to have the right attitude. It was wholly appropriate that it was raining when we first played in Nashville, as clearly it's a bad idea to let the weather affect your plans. To my best mate, Tom Covington, it was an unreal trip to Japan with the watermelon, baby. As was Sand Hills, and New Zealand, and Australia, and England, and the original trip to Garland with the Punjab. Looking forward to playing Morfontaine together one day with the wives! To my dear friend whose handicap has always been incorrect, Smythe, thank you for giving the gift that kept on giving; you created a monster. Little did we know what your simple gift would turn into. We have experienced the best together including the dream day at Cypress Point and your blowup at Pine Valley. Thank you for helping me through my mini-stroke in Paris and through my mini meltdown at Royal Birkdale. Fore left, that thing's going to blow up! You really should see a physician and have them look at your snoring problem. Many thanks to the good-looking Schlog who swings like an animal. Your sense of humor and forthright approach are a unique combination, and thank you for introducing me to the Bolivars and Clynelishes. I am glad we were able to play the Arran Course and the Budden Links together and got to enjoy the lovely Bordeaux. It's in the Marine Hotel.

To Roger, thank you for including me on your special trip to France with Fran, Danielle, and Mark. Your storytelling and knowledge of the game have added another dimension to our trips. Chambers, thank you for the invite to that first wild trip to Ireland, it was a life-changing experience and your attitude is infectious, mate.

I am not revealing the full name and clubs of most of my hosts out of respect for their privacy and so someone doesn't get the cute idea of trying to contact them to see if they can host them for a round of golf.

Countless thanks go to the myriad of people who were generous in hosting me or in helping me arrange rounds, beginning with my Chicago crew of Jim, Brad, Jack, Adams, Eric, and the "Sand Man." Special thanks to the Southerners: James, Suzanne, Rob, Mike, Mark, Carol, and John. And to Jon (going to school in the South counts). In Atlanta thanks to Brian, Al P., and Richard. On the West Coast thanks to Grandma, Uncle Dino, Mr. Langley, Damien and Mike in the Bay Area, as well as Papejoy, Jolly, Dave, and Steven in Southern California. Balan, your assistance is appreciated over the years as an editor and a friend. To David Krall and Schultzie, thank you for the debaucheries of our round at Riviera. To my friends north of the border, thank you to Stephen and Ben for being such gracious hosts.

In the Hamptons many thanks to Gus, you are a true gentleman and have been most gracious. And to Alec, Jack, and Don for your assistance at the National and Mid Ocean. And to Adam, John S., Jim B., and Tim as well as to Bob Murray and Brian Taylor. In Westchester thank you to Miniman, Brian, and James E., and to the generous invitation from Matthew. Thank you to Putter Boy and Jay Wood for showing me the rules of Connecticut golf: good-good. To Mitch and the H.R. lady, thank you for introducing me to the world-class Whip and Mo Howard. To my friends that helped in New Jersey and Philly especially Gino, John O., and Jack H., and to the folks at Merion Golf Club, who set the standard for excellence in the golf world. And to Stephanie Whittier: Who's better than you? No one!

For unparalleled assistance in Japan thank you Hiro and John, there is no way we could have pulled off such a great trip without you. In New England I would be remiss without mentioning D. Sears and his signature bow ties and a world-class sand game played in corduroys. To Dr. Phinney, heir to the Jergens Lotion Empire, thank you for all your help. In the Midwest, Plains, and Mountain West additional thanks to Fergal and Carl T., Jim H., Chester, Dan T., Larry F., Mark Q. and Tom W., Randy W., Tom G. and Tom H., as well as Joey Smith. Thanks to Graylyn Loomis for his editorial assistance and remember me when you are elected as R & A captain one day. Steve

DeWalle, keep up the great work on the site. Jamie and Michael, I hope you didn't peak too soon, the odds of that are still 88–1 on Slambino with the squeaky shoes.

Heaps of praise to Nancy Stulack at the USGA for her assistance and knowledge. And thanks again to the Royal Melbourne Golf Club for your generosity. And to the Greywalls and North Berwick for your permission to use your fabulous photographs.

Final thanks to Brian Lewis for his encouragement and thoughtful input; you have made a meaningful contribution to the game with your publishing efforts. And to my editorial team at Skyhorse, especially Julie Ganz and Deborah Goemans, for your thoughtful inputs. And to the most professional "Dee Dee" Crump-Durand, that's what he say. And to Maura, *bon chance* and thanks for all your support.

MacKenzie's sharp bunkering, Royal Melbourne West, 5th hole.

Bibliography

Legendary Golf Clubs of the American East, Anthony Edgeworth and John de St. Jorre, Edgeworth Editions, 2003.

Legendary Golf Clubs of Scotland, England, Wales and Ireland, Edgeworth Editions, 1999.

The World's 500 Greatest Golf Holes, George Peper, Artisan, 2003.

The Confidential Guide to Golf Courses, Tom Doak, Sleeping Bear Press, 1996.

The Confidential Guide to Golf Courses, Tom Doak, Renaissance Golf Design, 1994.

Planet Golf: The Definitive Reference to Great Golf Courses Outside the United States of America, Darius Oliver, Harry N. Abrams Inc., 2007.

Zen Golf, Dr. Joseph Parent, Doubleday, 2002.

The Luck Factor, Richard Wiseman, Miramax, 2003.

Down the Fairway, O.B. Keeler and Bobby Jones, Minton Balch, 1927.

The Power of Positive Thinking, Dr. Norman Vincent Peale, 1992.

Following Through, Herbert Warren Wind, Tichnor & Fields, 1985.

The Best of Henry Longhurst, Henry Longhurst, Collins, 1979.

The World Atlas of Golf, Pat Ward-Thomas, Gallery Books, 1976.

Two Years in St. Andrews: At Home on the 18th, George Peper, Simon & Schuster, 2006.

St. Andrews: How to Play the Old Course, Desmond Muirhead and Tip Anderson, Newport Press, 2000.

The Life and Work of Dr. Alister MacKenzie, Tom Doak, Dr. James S. Scott, and Raymund M. Haddock, Sleeping Bear Press, 2001.

Papwa Sewgolum: From Pariah to Legend, Chris Nicholson, Wits University Press, 2005.

The Durban Country Club 1918–1965, Peter Wrinch-Schulz, Wits University Press, 1965.

Souvenirs de Morfontaine, Jean Dulot, Editions Horarius & Co, 1998.

Chronique 1930–1999 Au Revoir Morfontaine . . . Merci, Editions Horarius & Co, 2000.

The First Forty One Years: A Tribute from The Augusta National Golf Club, Cliff Roberts, 1948.

Golf Is My Game, Bobby Jones, Doubleday & Company, 1960.

USGA Walker Cup Program, 1981 and *USGA Walker Cup Program,* 1985.

The Links, John De St. Jorre and Anthony Edgeworth, Edgeworth Editions, 2004.

Playing the Best Courses: Great Golf in the British Isles, Sir Peter Allen, Stanley Paul, 1973.

Golf My Way, Jack Nicklaus, Simon & Schuster, 2007.

The American Private Golf Club Guide, Daniel Wexler, MT III Golf Media, 2010.

Great Golf Courses of the World, Harper & Row, 1974.

The History of Sunningdale Golf Club 1900–2000, John Whitfield, Old Bakehouse Publications, 2000.

National Geographic Magazine, "Playing 3,000 Golf Courses in Fourteen Lands," July 1952.

The Times-Picayune, "Girdling the Globe for Golf," October 20, 1982.

The Times-Picayune, "Par Excellence: Global Golfer Shoots 100," July 30, 1986.

USGA Journal and Turf Management, "The Dr. Livingstone of Golf," November 1951.

The Links, 1955 Handbook.

The New York Post, "Nothin' but the Best for this Golf 'Nut'," July 25, 1999.

The New York Times, "Leading British Open Scores," July 11, 1963.

The New York Times, "Gary Player Ties for Second," February 1, 1965.

Pine Valley Golf Club 1969 Membership Handbook.

2010 United States Census, Hooker County, Nebraska, and Mullen, Nebraska.

Form 990, Return of Organization Exempt from Income Tax, 2004 and 2010, Cypress Point Club, Seminole Golf Club, Merion Golf Club, Chicago Golf Club, Fishers Island Club, The Los Angeles Country Club.

Travel and Leisure Golf Magazine, January 2006.

The Swinley Special, Nicholas Courtney, Phillimore, 2008.

The Architectural Record, July-December 1917.

Scotland's Gift, Charles Blair Macdonald, Scribner's Sons, 1928.

The Wall Street Journal, "O'Neal Out as Merrill Reels from Loss," October 27, 2007.

Bloomberg, Michael Lewis, "O'Neal's Agony, or, In the Bunker with Stan," November 6, 2007.

New York Times, "Where Did the Buck Stop at Merrill?" November 4, 2007 and "The O'Neal Weekend Watch: He's Gone," October 26, 2007.

Links Magazine, March 2006, May/June 2006.

Global News, Robert Thompson, "Canada's Most Exclusive Golf Courses you May Never Get to Play," June 16, 2014.

The Rolex World's Top 1000 Golf Courses, First Edition, 2010.

Shadow Creek, Steve Winn, 1995.

Las Vegas Sun. "Shadow Creek Golf Course: Where Not Even the President Can Get a Tee Time," April 6, 2013.

*ESPN.*com, "Fan Gives Double-eagle Ball to Club," April 9, 2012.

The A Position, "By Donating an Albatross Ball, Masters Patron receives notable perks," May 2012.

The Architectural Side of Golf, H. W. Wethered and Tom Simpson, Ailsa, 2001.

Ellis Island Passenger Record, April 30, 1913, North German Lloyd, Berlin, Naples, Campania, Italy.

*Masters.*com, "Augusta's Elevation Changes Surprise First-Timers," April 1, 2011.

Great Golf Courses of the World, Herbert Warren Wind, titled "The Architect Makes a Great Golf Course," 1974.

Golf Course at Pocantico Hills, the Estate of John V. Rockefeller, Jr., USGA Museum Collection.

*GolfClubAtlas.*com, "Pocantico Hills, Impossible Access??" W.S. Morrison, March 27, 2007.

Ralph Kennedy Scrapbooks, USGA Museum, 1917–1932, 1932–1936, 1936–1940, 1940–1946, 1946–1951, 1951–1955.

The Making of the Masters, David Owen, Simon & Schuster, 1999.

The Toronto Terror: The Life and Works of Stanley Thompson, Golf Course Architect, James A. Barclay, Sleeping Bear Press, 2000.

Portraits: Early members of Augusta National Golf Club, Augusta National, 1962.

Ike, Golf & Augusta, David Sowell, 2012.

Dwight D. Eisenhower Presidential Library and Museum. Abilene, Kansas. "Correspondence related to Morfontaine Golf Club 1951–1952."

Golf Digest, "Land of the Rising Golfer," October 1962.

Index

Photo Credits

About the Author

John Sabino is among a small group of golfers who have achieved the feat of playing the top 100 ranked golf courses in the world, a list as small as the number of men who have been to the moon. John chronicled his journey around the world to complete his quest in a blog www.top100golf.blogspot.com, that has over 1 million readers. In addition, he has been featured in *Links Magazine, Australian Golf Digest, The Star Ledger, The Wall Street Journal, Golf Digest Index, Luxury Travel Magazine,* and *Billionaire Magazine.* An avid golfer and student of golf history, John brings an unparalleled enthusiasm, a unique perspective, and an insider's insight to the task. John makes his living in the financial services industry and lives in the golf-rich state of New Jersey, home to the number one ranked golf course in the world and the United States Golf Association.